Do You *truly* Know Him?

Or Just Know *about* Him?

© Copyright 2024-Matcine Pepper

All rights reserved. Permission is granted to copy or reprint portions for any noncommercial use, except they may not be posted online without permission.

Wyatt & Sons Publishers books may be ordered through booksellers or by contacting:

Wyatt & Sons Publishers, LLC
Mobile, Alabama 36695
www.wyattpublishing.com
editor@wyattpublishing.com

Because of the dynamic nature of the Internet, any web address or links contained in this book may have changed since publication and may no longer be valid.

Unless otherwise indicated, all scripture references are Scripture taken from the New King James Version®.Copyright © 1982 by Thomas Nelson. Used by permission. All rights reserved.

Cover illustration by: Jessica Smith
Cover design by: Sam Noerr
Interior design by: Mark Wyatt

ISBN 13:978-1-954798-25-0
Printed in the United States of America

Do You *truly* Know Him?

Or Just Know *about* Him?

by
Matcine Pepper

WYATT & SONS
PUBLISHERS, LLC
Mobile, Alabama

TABLE OF CONTENTS

Acknowledgments		7
What People Are Saying About This Book		16
Suggestions For The Reader		21

SECTION I: IN THE BEGINNING

1	A Man's Heart Plans His Way	25
	Unconditional Love	*30*
2	Be As Wise As A Serpent	31
3	Who Am I That You Are Mindful Of Me	34
4	Many Are The Afflictions Of The Righteous	38
5	My Testimony Of Hope Restored	45
6	Posture Your Heart	49
7	Reveal Anything In My Heart That Is Not Of You	52
8	Saved From My Sin	54
9	Submit To God	55
10	Thank You For Making A Way Of Escape	61
11	Your Birth Gave Me Life And Purpose	65

Section II: JOURNEY TO WHOLENESS

1	A New Life Has Begun	73
2	A Prayer To Abide In God	80
3	Awaken You Who Slumber	83
4	Don't Conform, Be Transformed	87
5	Dwell And Abide	92
6	Illuminate All Darkness	95
7	In My Weakness You Are Made Strong	98
8	Obedience Is Better Than Sacrifice	101
9	The Lord Of The Ring	104
10	Wait Upon The Lord	107
11	Your Love Knows No Bounds	110

Section III: SALVATION, DELIVERANCE AND FREEDOM

1	A Light Will Shine	115
2	Do You Know The Resurrection	118
3	Don't Let Your Heart Be Troubled	123
4	He Who Promised Is Faithful	128
5	Holy Spirit, Help Those Who Are Hurting Learn How To Trust You	131
6	Lord, Please Open My Eyes	134
7	New Home And Job Loss Testimony	136
8	Ready Or Not, He's Coming Soon	139
9	The Good Shepherd	142
10	Do You Truly Know Him	145

FINAL THOUGHTS   *150*

ACKNOWLEDGMENTS

First and foremost, I would like to thank my Heavenly Father, for His patience, unconditional love, and for His Spirit who dwells in me, who helps me live and move and have my being in Him. Without God's love in my life, this book would never have come into being. He birthed it in me before the foundations of the earth.

Now, it is obvious why my life was always such a struggle and seemed hopeless. But, the Greater One who lives in me saw that I was never defeated and He will never let me fail.

As I have grown to know Him more intimately over the last few years, I can see that these messages He put in my heart to share were messages from His heart to mine, but also messages to share with every person destined to read this book. He not only wants me to know how much he loves me, but for all to know how much he loves us, and how far He will go to grow us up in our faith and our relationships with Him.

He is an intentional God; nothing takes place by mistake. The one thing He wants from us once we receive Him as the Lord of our lives is to surrender to Him. When we are surrendered and no longer seeking our will; when our hearts are opened to what He desires for us; being teachable, humble, and willing to die to self, the possibilities with God are limitless.

You will then discover gifts and talents you may have never known you had, or you will focus on sharpening the ones you know about. His gifts are always Kingdom-oriented. He blesses us to be a blessing to others so that they too can have hope, seeing that His love is boundless and filled with much more than we could ever ask or think of. He knows the plans He has for us, and as we yield our lives to Him, we will walk with Him in a way we never knew was possible; fulfilling and being fulfilled. That is what a life in Christ will do for you when you finally understand what it means to truly know Him, and no longer just know about Him. I love You, Jesus!

I would also like to thank my husband, Harvey. Ever since God revealed to me that I was to write a book, he has stood by my side to support me. There have been many ups and downs during this process; times of discouragement from setbacks, and many exciting milestones, as I've had to learn the ins and outs of book writing. These experiences have been valuable lessons and brought us excitement and joy, in the setbacks and delays. At the end of the day no matter what we faced, he stood by my side and covered me in prayer through every challenge before us. Thank you, Harvey, for standing by my side. I love you!

The next person in my heart to thank is my spiritual mother and mentor, Sherry. Without her love, prayers, obedience, commitment to God first, and belief in me when I didn't believe in myself, this book would likely never have happened. She helped to nurture me spiritually during one of the darkest times of my life. She gave me Holy Ghost CPR and helped to jumpstart my empty and dying heart.

After helping me discover I didn't truly know Him, I repented of my sin and recommitted my heart to Jesus. I have journeyed with Him closer in my walk since; learning who He is in me, and who I am in Him. Thank you, Sherry, for loving me as a daughter and teaching by example how to be free in Jesus. Thank you for the countless prayers, and unconditional love; for correcting and rebuking me when I need it; for the many ways you show you care for and love me as Jesus does; for holding me accountable, and for not backing down or compromising on anything. Thank you for the many laughs and the many tears we've shared. Thank you for being my sounding board and allowing me to share my life with you; for always encouraging me to look to Jesus for what concerns me regarding my family, this book, and many other concerns.

I am eternally grateful to God for knitting our hearts together and for you pointing me to Him always; for helping me to see He has a plan for my life. I give Him all of the glory for what He has done. Thank you for being the yielded and obedient vessel He chose to use, so His plan and purpose for my life could begin to take root and blossom to its fullness. Everyone needs a mentor who is so selfless to sow into their lives. May He bless you above and beyond all you can ask or think of! I love you!

My amazing and beautiful book coach and now precious friend, Rae Lynne Johnson, thank you! The many hours of Zoom calls and for your expertise in writing and understanding the ins and outs of making a good book exceptional thank you; for always greeting me with a smile and a heart that genuinely cares about her clients, thank you; for beginning and ending most every meeting in prayer and for seeing God in the big and little achievements, thank you; for being patient, encouraging, understanding, gentle yet firm; for going the extra mile for me when you did not have to, thank you; for making the time to edit in your already busy schedule, and for pointing out to me that I was over-using exclamation marks, thank you!! Sorry, I couldn't resist! LOL

This whole project has been quite an experience for me, and I will always cherish the time God used you in such an impactful way in my life. You are truly a treasure to rising writers and a blessing in my life personally. I am beyond thankful for God sending you to me as I searched for someone to help me make His plan for this book happen.

I look forward to hugging your neck soon, should Jesus tarry. I could say much more, but this forward has already turned into another book, and there are still others to thank. I love you!

I would like to give special thanks to Jessica Smith, the amazing artist who sketched and charcoaled the beautiful cover photo of Jesus. I never imagined when I won an auction for the drawing of this breathtaking piece of art on social media, I would be using it for the cover of this book. God was overseeing every step of this book, and I remember Him clearly saying, "This is your book cover" after it arrived in the mail. I am blessed and honored to be the vessel He chose to make this book happen. But, without the anointed and gifted talent of Jessica Smith, this book would not have its intended effect on those who are destined to read it.

Thank you, Jessica, for allowing me the honor of using the beautiful picture of Jesus for my book. Your hand in this will touch many lives beyond anything you or I can imagine. I pray those who appreciate your gift will search you out on Facebook, or Etsy at:(JessicaSmithArtShop.Etsy.com), and that you will flourish in all that you give your hands to, to the glory of God. Many blessings to you and your precious family. You are loved.

I would also like to give photo credit to Terry Windquist. Thank you for offering to take my bio photo when I first mentioned that I was writing a book. Your offer blessed me and I was thankful when I could take you up on it. Choosing the best photo was hard, but I think I made the right choice. It was a fun time and I am blessed and honored that you took time out of your schedule to do that for me. I highly recommend anyone looking for a wonderful photographer to look you up. I love you!

I would like to give a big shout out to Sam Noerr for his graphic artistic abilities. After me expressing to you what I was looking for, you ran with it and did not disappoint, whatsoever. As much as the title of the book is important, I wanted the face of Jesus to be the main focus and for nothing to draw the eyes away from Him. As the whole purpose of this book is to make people question, *Do I Truly Know Him? Or just know about Him?* The textured cover and the simple lined frame as well as the font selection is perfect! Thank you sir, I believe in my heart, Jesus is going to be proud of the whole outcome of this amazing work.

And finally, last but certainly not least, many other special people have supported, encouraged, and prayed for me during this writing journey:

I would like to thank Angela for standing by me through all of the ups and downs of this writing experience. For praying for me and encouraging me even while you were battling with serious health issues. Thank you for always believing in me and never giving up on me. I love you!

I am thankful for my beautiful niece, Lori, for all of your support, love, and help around my house, and yard; for letting me share many of my writings with you, and for your sharp eye for editing and finding mistakes to help this book be the best it can be. Thank you for loving me and for believing in me! Thank you also for letting me use your printer for my manuscript. I am honored to call you my niece and my sister in Christ! I am blessed watching you flourish with God in your life, and I can hardly wait to see all He has in store for you. Thank you for standing by my side through this writing journey. Keep sowing into others lives and He will bless you in ways you never imagined He would. I love you!

Thank you, to my sister, Mary Alice. Thank you for your prayers, love, and support, as you have been my #1 supporter over the years where my writings are concerned. The apple didn't fall far from the tree, because you, my sister (not by blood only, but in Christ too), have quite a gift to write and to express God's heart. I pray you will consider taking some special time to write more and see how God inspires you. Do it for His glory. This is a gift He gave us both. I know you will fully grasp His purpose for creating you before the earth was formed or came into existence when you start writing what's in His heart. I love you!

I would also like to thank Elaine, Susan, and Sherry, for encouraging me to write God's book. It took me a little while to grasp that He had placed a book in me, but with your help, I finally saw it! Thank you for believing in me and praying during this challenging but rewarding journey. I am forever grateful for your love, prayers, support, and your friendship in Christ. I love each of you dearly.

Special thank you goes to Mark Wyatt, of Wyatt & Sons Publishers, LLC. Mark has been a friend for about fifteen years. I was first introduced to him as a pastor, as I searched for a church open to allowing the Holy Spirit to move; one that operated in signs, wonders, and miracles. This church checked all of our boxes, and then some. He had a way of preaching and teaching the Word of God in a way that makes you hungry for more. We both had roots that started in another local church but didn't know each other then. He is very gifted, creative, and has a great imagination. He has a heart for God and those who need to experience his love. He is married to his beautiful wife, Mary Ann, and they have 4 children, a son and daughter-in-law, and 3 precious grandsons.

If anyone is writing a book and needs a publisher who will handle their manuscript with the utmost care, be efficient, and have their book ready for print in a reasonable time, I highly recommend Wyatt and Sons Publishers.

Thank you, Carol Williams, for helping to edit the devotional portion of the book. Your willingness and heart to help blessed me and I appreciate your kindness. May God richly bless you and all that you put your hands to. I love you.

There are many others to thank, but I cannot thank everyone without leaving someone out. If you prayed for me during these last two years for God's wisdom, guidance, protection, or provision, or any other reason; if you offered me an encouraging word, a hug, or a blessing, you know who you are, and from the bottom of my heart, I say, thank you. You are all loved and so much appreciated.

I pray this book will bless each of you, and thank God for the special place you each hold in my heart. I also pray for all who will set aside time to read this devotional book and work the journal, that your hearts will be blessed beyond anything you expected it could be. God's heart is for you and He longs to have a deep, intimate relationship with each of us. This book, if read as it needs to be, will help you to achieve this desire the Father has for you, and in turn will cause you to walk in His fullness, for the remainder of your days on earth. You will then walk in full assurance of being able to say, Yes, I Truly Know Him! God bless you. You are loved!

What people are saying about this book...

"God's grace for Matcine shines through her book. As her journey of affliction echoes through her words, it is evident how she daily walked down a very personal and abiding love with the Father.

Each chapter is an opportunity for the reader to draw closer to God through self-reflection, self-honesty, and self-transparency.

I encourage everyone no matter where they are on their journey with God, to dive deep into this book with the expectation that their walk with God will grow deeper and wider than ever before."

—*Ellis Noone*

"This journal is truly from the heart of the Father, through this author's once-shattered life. She was transformed into a beautiful butterfly. When God finished His work in her, she became a most beautiful pearl made by God's healing hands as a gift to us.

Through God's will, this book was birthed, so that we could be restored to the truth of who Father really is in the new birth; we will come to know Him and not just about Him.

I promise you, Holy Spirit will refine you to come to a place within, that you will honestly know Him in such intimacy that you will become just like Him. Yes exactly like He intended.

Through these wonderful writings, you will be healed in your heart, mind, soul, emotions, and spirit.

Be blessed and learn who you are in Christ, and then you can say, yes, I know You, Jesus."

—*Sherry Primley*

"'Do you truly know Him?'

What a question! Loaded, no doubt. Thought-provoking, offensive, scandalous even, is this five-word sentence. Matcine Pepper has not only lived through an amazing journey to answer this question herself, but she has gifted the readers of this wonderfully written and well-laid-out devotional with an incredible opportunity to go deeper within themselves to find out the truth about how well they truly know God.

As the author and guide of this book, Mrs. Pepper shares her testimony of her need for answers and the questions that she asked God during one of the lowest points of her life, which led her on a mission to find out more about her Creator and the many facets He possesses.

Her quest culminated with amazing revelations, a relationship with the Father she'd always dreamed of, and a deep desire to help others who were also questioning God and looking for the same answers.

This devotional will challenge you, awaken you, and create a deeper hunger and thirst for God as you journal your thoughts and press into His arms like never before. By the time you reach the last page, you'll be closer to God than ever and eager to share your experiences with others as the writer has! Get ready to go deeper and truly KNOW God."

—Tracie Mark Smith, Chaplain
Recovery Coach/Teacher

"As I began to move through this devotional/journal I soon realized it read more like a 'Field Manual' for all who desire to draw closer in their relationship with God.

Beautifully and thoughtfully written, "Do You Truly Know Him" is a foundational study and reminder of God's prevailing word and presence in our lives. The personal testimonies written with such transparency and the transformative scriptures reminding us of God's majesty and love, no doubt set the reader on a sure and faithful path in deepening their relationship with God.

I highly recommend this devotional for all who seek to know HIM in a deeper and more abiding way. May Holy Spirit touch each of us as we scour over the divinely inspired pages of this instructional 'Field Manual'. May many students of the word pick this up and become more intimate with the knowledge of the Almighty."

—Mrs. Tami Lightfoot
Co-Founder, Victory Health Partners

"This is a five-star book. If I could give it more stars I would. I can't say enough to encourage everyone to read these amazing words! I must say I have never read anything like it.

I couldn't wait to read each day the things I would have never asked myself about God or questioned God about; the way I pray, things I have never thought to ask God for or about.

Each page teaches something, and I love the question-and-answer part in the companion journal pages. They open your eyes to see exactly what we should be asking ourselves.

As you read deeper into this teaching, you experience God more intimately. Learning to hear Him speak to you is encouraging and keeps you wanting to read more.

I'm so blessed to have read these words. I can't explain my true feelings about this book the Holy Spirit guided Matcine Pepper to write. Without it, I would have never learned what I have been taught through this devotional and journal.

Thank you, Holy Spirit and Matcine. God speaks to me in many ways now. I have become a different person after reading the insight that flows out of these words. God truly loves us and wants us to know who He is. This book will help you to truly know Him."

—*Trish Wilson*

Suggestions for the Reader

Before I make any suggestions, I would like to give a heartfelt thank you to all who are seeking to know "Do I Truly Know Him?"

The writing of this devotional and companion journal first came to me as a burden the Lord placed on my heart. I didn't understand these were messages He wanted me to put out there for others. I was studying and endeavoring to grow in my walk with Him by using the YouVersion Bible App to help me grow more disciplined in my Bible study and prayer time. As I read the Scripture of the Day, or scriptures in the Guided Prayer section, I sometimes felt compelled to write a thought as a "Prayer" or "Encouraging Word." As I began writing, the idea would turn into much more than that. It would go from a mere thought to something I often did not fully understand. Before I knew it, I had a full page of what I felt were my thoughts along with scriptures. Then, I later understood that they were inspired revelations given to me by The Holy Spirit.

I believe the things I've written were for me initially but also for me to share with others. Facebook became my platform for sharing these messages from the Lord. As I started posting more, people would express to me how God was touching them and speaking to their hearts through my posts. Some friends started asking me when I was going to write a book. I never set out to write a book and knew nothing about writing books. But, before I knew it, I was talking with my Book Coach about plans for my first book.

God has directed almost every step of this book, except where I tried to go ahead of Him out of my zealousness to finish it. He gave me the title and helped me come up with the cover, not realizing the picture would be a cover photo when I "won it in an auction." He sent my Book Coach to me, and with her help, patience, and much grace, she has walked me through the completion of this journey.

It has been an honor and a privilege to be used as a vessel to bring glory to God. I pray as you go through each day's reading, God will speak to your hearts and reveal something new about Him you did not know. As you learn about who He is in an even deeper way, I pray He will also reveal things about yourself you didn't know. This book and the journal are to be used as tools to help you grow stronger in your Christian walk, or in some cases, as you discover, maybe "I" don't truly know Him, you will surrender your heart to Him and make Jesus Lord of your life so that you can truly know Him.

Although this book is designed as a 32-day devotional and journal, please don't feel the need to rush through. (Why 32 days—I "accidentally" added an extra one and couldn't decide which one to remove.) It is not your typical devotional with condensed writings, and some days may require you to do a lot of reflection as God speaks to your heart. When you use the companion journal for each day, this will require some thought to help God unlock some things in you that He may want to open your eyes to. I ask that you approach this with an open heart to receive all God wants to open your eyes to see and your heart to receive. May you walk away from reading this book and journal enriched and strengthened as a Child of God, knowing He has brought this book to you to prepare you as a believer for the days ahead. May God richly bless every reader, I pray, in Jesus' name. Amen.

In the beginning...

A MAN'S HEART PLANS HIS WAY

Five years ago we bought a new home. Less than two weeks later, I fell in my garage and broke my neck. A month to the day from signing the closing documents and taking ownership of our home, I lost my job. I was overwhelmed with the turn of events in my life.

Because I was misdiagnosed, I didn't know I broke my neck until four months later. It is by the grace of God I'm still alive. I had surgery to fuse my head and neck using a titanium plate and two rods extending from the base of my skull to the C6 vertebrae. After a prolonged recovery, I believed the lie from the enemy that I was of no use to God; He was done with me. Though I was thankful to be alive, I spiraled into depression, knowing I was limited in the things I could do.

With four children and their spouses, and at last count, sixteen beautiful grandchildren, the Lord has blessed me. I have much to be thankful for. However, this accident changed the direction of my life. With limited mobility in my neck, I felt I would not be much fun for my grandchildren. There would be less time playing and interacting with them as I was used to doing. I also felt I would be limited in the help I could give my family, such as babysitting or cooking meals. I'm very thankful and blessed to be alive so I can be involved with their lives. I may have limited time with them, but I am thankful for each moment I'm able to enjoy spending time with them.

Everything that happens serves as a stepping stone to make us stronger in Christ. Without trials and tribulations, sickness, a job loss, a damaged friendship, and many other possibilities, we would never see any need to call out to Jesus. Leaning on Him in the good and bad times strengthens us through all trials. As we look back over times of testing in our lives, we see how He was there to help us through.

We can then testify of His faithfulness to keep His Word and promises to those who love Him and follow Him. As we testify of our victories over trials, we give others hope that if He "gave us victories, He will do it for them too." Testimonies of His love and faithfulness keep others from losing hope and give them a desire to trust Him all the more.

A few months after falling and breaking my neck, God brought a precious sister into my life, an acquaintance on social media. She had begun interceding for me in prayer when she saw a photo of me in my neck brace. We started communicating and soon became close friends. We have kindred spirits, and she has loved and encouraged me in so many ways. She became the hands and feet of Jesus in my life. Although she lives over two thousand miles away, there is no distance in the Spirit. She has helped me see that God is anything but done with me. He is just beginning with me. She has supported me in prayer through many hardships and has been a compass in my life to help point me to Jesus, my True North.

We have laughed and cried together. Through her example, she shows me how to grow stronger in my walk with Him. Her love for Jesus is like none I've ever seen. She is my mentor and Spiritual Mother, and I am eternally grateful God brought her into my life and has woven our hearts together.

Because of her and a few other special people in my life, this book is even possible. I've never had anyone encourage or believe in me, or hold me accountable the way she has. I only pray I will be half the disciple of Jesus she is when my life is done! I honor her, and I know God is pleased with her. She is the real deal; devils run when they see her coming.

Now, instead of seeing myself as washed up, I know I have purpose. God's plan is greater than I could have imagined or dreamed. I thank Him for His gifts and callings, and I pray He is honored through this work.

Whether we are in the valley or on the mountaintop, if we are walking with God, He is directing our steps. Trust that He is working all things for our good as we stay on the straight and narrow path He has for us. We will endure trials and tests. Keeping our eyes on Him as we go through the trials will make us stronger when we come out on the other side.

God has given me the gift of writing and expressing His heart of love through my experiences and His inspirations. These writings started in the form of poems that express many of my life experiences. Then through reading scriptures in my quiet time, His Spirit inspires me with encouraging words and prayers to bring hope to others through these writings.

The poem following this testimony was the first one I wrote, and it touches on where I was, emotionally and spiritually during this time in my life. It's hard to believe that person was me! I have been transformed into a very different person. I truly believe this poem has the power to help others who are walking where I was at the time, or in similar situations. It was inspired by The Holy Spirit and will bring life to you if you are open to receiving it.

My prayer is that all of the poems and other writings I share are used mightily by God for His glory. They will help break strongholds in your life, dispelling every lie the enemy of your soul has tried to make you believe.

"Who the Son makes free is free indeed!" (John 8:36)

It is an honor and a blessing to be used by God to express His love through the things He inspires me to write. I pray you experience the love of Jesus and the freedom of His shed blood for you on the cross, as you read these passages. I love you and pray the messages written will reveal to you how much God loves you too!

I also pray for all who read the companion journal to be challenged to reflect on their journey through life and their relationship with the Lord, asking the question, "Do I truly know Him?" If not, seek Him and know He wants to show you how much your True Love and Bridegroom loves you. He has much to show you before He returns for His Bride soon. Go after Him with all of your heart, soul, and strength. Acknowledge your need, and I promise you will never regret it.

"And they overcame him (satan) by the blood of the Lamb (Jesus) and by the word of their testimony, and they did not love their lives to the death." (Revelation 12:11)

"Oh, taste and see that the Lord is good; Blessed is the man/woman who trusts in Him!" (Psalms 34:8)

In Jesus' love,
Matcine Pepper

UNCONDITIONAL LOVE

There have been times in my deepest despair,
I was not sure that God was there.
As my heart ached, I did not know,
If I prayed to Him, He would lift me so.

I thought, since forgiven for all of my sins,
I would never get down and would always win.
Although He forgave me long ago,
I forgave not myself, I could not let go!

But now since I've come to see The Light,
He's lifted my heart with all of His might.
I give Him the glory for my precious life,
My Heavenly Father has removed all my strife.

He is my Creator, this I know,
He loves and accepts me and helps me to grow.
I pray that you know our Father above,
So that you too can know Unconditional Love!

Inspired by Holy Spirit through
Matcine Pepper
1991

BE AS WISE AS A SERPENT

There is a reason the Lord instructs us to be as wise as serpents, yet as harmless as doves. To be wise as serpents requires us to know the Word of God and how to apply it in any situation we face.

Satan and his demons know God's Word well. They have been given rule over the earth and will use anything they can to destroy God's plans for our lives. Any weakness in our faith and lack of understanding of God's Word sets us up as a target for him to try to destroy us. They know if we understand who we are in Christ and believe who He is in us. If we are powerless in our faith because we don't know God's Word, satan, like a lion, is ready to devour us. He will do anything or use anyone to keep us dumbed down and weak. He also knows when we've learned who we are in Christ and the authority we have over him. He then knows he can no longer keep us down or prevent us from fulfilling God's call on our lives.

If we love Jesus, we should seek Him by reading His Word, praying, and worshiping Him. If we are not doing these things, we are either passively walking hand-in-hand with satan or being pummeled by him. In either case, in our impotence, we pose no threat to him.

Friends, this is a spiritual battle we are fighting. If we want to walk in victory over the realms of darkness, we must armor up daily by reading the Bible, praying, and worshiping Jesus (spiritual weapons of warfare.) Get in the battle, and fight against every demonic force coming against you, your family, and those who don't yet know how to stand and fight.

Our struggle is not against flesh and blood; however, the enemy can use those closest to us to come against us. Many play right into his hand: blinded, deceived, and bewitched by the enemy because they lack knowledge of the spiritual realm. Ask for wisdom and discernment for them. Pray for God to open their spiritual eyes to see that He will deliver and set them free. We must still take our authority over the demons operating in them so they don't cause us to shrink back out of fear. Be as bold as a lion!

Being as wise as a serpent, we must hear from God how to beat the enemy at his own game. Being as harmless as a dove, we must love the person being misused, praying for them and trusting God's power to deliver them from their tormentors.

"For we do not wrestle against flesh and blood, but against principalities, against powers, against the rulers of the darkness of this age, against spiritual hosts of wickedness in the heavenly places."

Ephesians 6:12

"Therefore if the Son makes you free, you shall be free indeed."

John 8:36

"Behold, I send you out as sheep in the midst of wolves. Therefore, be wise as serpents and harmless as doves."

Matthew 10:16

WHO AM I THAT YOU ARE MINDFUL OF ME

"You are worthy, O Lord, To receive glory and honor and power; For You created all things, And by Your will they exist and were created."

Revelation 4:11

Father, Lord of heaven and earth, and all within them, I humbly bow before You and proclaim, You are my God, the very One who created my being. In all of Your Splendor and Magnificence, You not only created the whole universe, but You created even finite me! One who is but a vapor in the vastness of Your beautiful Creation.

You made me out of the dust of the earth, and to the dust, my body will return when the end of my time has come. By Your design, I am anything but insignificant. Compared to You, I am nothing, and apart from You, I have no purpose whatsoever. My righteousness is like filthy rags. You alone can cleanse me and make me as white as snow.

You formed me with intricate detail, complete in every way. I was given Your DNA, yet You made me unique. You created all of my inward parts to work together, causing my body to function like a well-oiled clock with all its mechanisms working together in unison keeping it ticking and accurately telling time.

Each organ, each organism, each cell, every sinew, and each body part, all work together in unison, as You designed them to. You made me a female in Your image. You knew exactly what color my skin, hair, and eyes would be. You knew how tall I would be. You gave me my senses that I would hear, see, smell, taste, and feel in the natural.

You called me by name and knew everything about me before being conceived in my mother's womb. You created me with a womb to birth the lives of future generations and the heritage of those who come after me. You also knew them before the foundations of the earth. Each created with the same intricate detail, yet all unique and in Your image. All are formed and created for a specific purpose and born for such a time as this.

You created me with a soul; mind, will, and emotions. You gave me free will to choose, and You created me with a void within, that only You can fill. You also created me as a spirit. I am a spirit, I have a soul, and I live in a body. This body and my soul will one day perish, but my spirit will live throughout eternity, either in Heaven with You, or in hell with satan.

Although I was born in sin because of Adam and Eve's rebellion and disobedience, I do not have to die in sin and go to hell. Because the blood of Jesus was shed, and He gave His life, so Your Creation can live and have eternal life with You in Heaven. He paid the ultimate price for all mankind with His life because You love Your Creation. It's not Your will for any to perish, but that all have eternal life with You!

Thank You, Papa, for creating me, for redeeming my soul from the pit, for showing me I have value and am loved with an everlasting love by You! You know the number of my days. I know because of Your great love, I will one day join You and Your Son, and I will walk the streets of gold. I will never look back or even remember my former life, as I was delivered from my old nature when You came into my heart, and my life was made new. I will have a glorified body and live throughout eternity worshiping and praising Your Glorious name! O Lord, who am I that You are mindful of me?

"O Lord, our Lord, How excellent is Your name in all the earth, Who have set Your glory above the heavens! Out of the mouth of babes and nursing infants You have ordained strength, Because of Your enemies, That You may silence the enemy and the avenger. When I consider Your heavens, the work of Your fingers, The moon and the stars, which You have ordained, What is man that You are mindful of him, And the son of man that You visit him? For You have made him a little lower than the angels, And You have crowned him with glory

and honor. You have made him to have dominion over the works of Your hands; You have put all things under his feet, All sheep and oxen—Even the beasts of the field, The birds of the air, And the fish of the sea that pass through the paths of the seas. O Lord, our Lord, How excellent is Your name in all the earth!"

Psalms 8:1-9 NKJV

MANY ARE THE AFFLICTIONS OF THE RIGHTEOUS

"Many are the afflictions of the righteous, but the Lord delivers him out of them all."

Psalms 34:19

Lord, if the righteous have many afflictions, how much more do the unrighteous suffer? I know we all have different personalities, as well as life circumstances. If all I have suffered could be compared with the unsaved on a scale, there must be many whose lives are a living hell. For I know many have suffered much more than I have. We live in a fallen world, and none are exempt from the sufferings of this world.

As early as I can remember, I "felt" rejected and unloved. (Not that I was, it was a lie I believed). I'm convinced the spirit of rejection entered me while in the womb. I was the last of six children. My mother was older and tired, and likely unable to see how she could give birth to and raise one more child. She must have felt overwhelmed when she found out she was expecting again. She was then 38, with two-year-old twins. She already had her hands full. She may have had an initial response of shock and confusion, most likely inhibiting her joy. I don't know this to be a fact, however, I "felt" rejected and unloved most of my life. I know she took extreme measures to avoid miscarrying me, resting in bed for several months to avoid losing me.

The earliest lie I believed was part of satan's plan to keep me discouraged throughout my life. It came to me through a "spirit," and this was not the spirit of God. This "spirit" could have come through my mother's emotions when she found out she was expecting. It could have been passed down through a generational curse. It could have come another way also, but regardless of how it came, it was there and caused me to believe the lie, "Nobody loves me."

We are spiritual beings and are born under the curse that Jesus took for us on the cross. God's goodness is stronger than anything the enemy can do to us, but we are all influenced by something. We either walk in blessings or curses. If thoughts of dread, hate, or evil are emotions we express, the spirit of darkness has entered our hearts. Although babies are the most innocent of God's creation, the enemy will do everything in his power to impart his lies to all who will believe them, even in the mother's womb! The earlier he can start coming against us with his deception and lies, the more effective he can be at keeping us from fulfilling the purpose God created us for.

Although my parents most likely did not plan my birth, God did! I am not a mistake. No matter how I have perceived myself throughout life, it was God's plan for me to be here before He created the foundations of the world. No demon in hell can thwart the plans of God. They may temporarily succeed at slowing you down by causing you to feel worthless and of no significance, but with God's hand upon you, they can't continue to deceive you with their lies.

Don't be dismayed my friends, although satan is crafty in trying to destroy us, God has the last word. When Jesus died on the cross, he descended into the bowels of hell, disarming the devil of his power to destroy God's creation. He took the keys to death, hell, and the grave. Death has lost its sting because Jesus triumphed over death. We will all die a physical death, however, our spiritual bodies will live on. Where we live through all eternity depends on the choice we make before our physical bodies pass away. If we choose to invite Jesus to come into our lives, we will spend eternity with Him. Otherwise, we will spend eternity in torment and darkness. Never to have any hope of being free from the clutches of satan. Satan only has victory and power over those who give it to him by not receiving Jesus as their Lord and Savior.

Because of the power of the blood Jesus shed on the cross, God's children have the authority to walk in the victory of the cross. The cross and the blood Jesus shed bridged the gap sin causes between us and God. It gave

Lay your ideas about Christianity down and seek the heart of God. Humble yourself, let Him know you need Him to reveal Himself to you. He loves a broken and remorseful heart, humble and not proud. A heart willing to die daily to the world, the flesh, and the devil and to surrender all to Him.

Once you truly surrender, letting go of all that has kept you separated from God, His blessings will be released over your life. You will be completely amazed at His goodness and favor in your life. Walking a surrendered life isn't easy and it requires sacrifice, but the eternal rewards are worth sacrificing your life for, if necessary. That's what His Son did for every one of us, so who are we not to be willing to do the same?

"If God be for us, who can be against us?"
Romans 8:31b

"For He made Him who knew no sin to be sin for us, that we might become the righteousness of God in Him."
2 Corinthians 5:21

If you are empty, hopeless, and confused about whether you have a real purpose in life; if you desire more and want to walk in the fullness and blessings of God, call out to Him right where you are. Confess you are a sinner and that you need a Savior. Ask Him to forgive you for your sin, to cleanse you of all of the filth and the lies you have lived in and believed.

us power to walk in victory as we overcome every lie and deception of the enemy. When we testify, it's like us saying, "In your face devil, you no longer have the power to nullify the purpose of my life!"

"And they overcame him (satan) by the blood of the Lamb (Jesus) and by the word of their testimony, and they (you and me) did not love their lives to the death."
Revelation 12:11

You have power to choose to walk in victory if you know God! The question is, do you truly know Him, or just know about Him? When you truly know God, you have an intimate relationship with Him. You might have said a "sinners prayer" because you felt convicted, believing you became a "Christian." Saying the prayer does not transform you into a Christian.

The Spirit of God comes to set you free by giving you a new heart of repentance, giving you the desire to commit your life to Christ. Christ convicts you, then removes the darkness within you. Conviction leads us to repentance. Condemnation which comes from satan leads us to shame, making us feel hopeless and powerless to overcome sin and temptation. It makes us believe it depends on us to be good. But in our power, we are nothing and can do nothing. We are as filthy rags in our strength, but in Christ, we can do all things.

"I can do all things through Christ who strengthens me."

Philippians 4:13

be at keeping us from fulfilling the purpose God created us for.

Although my parents most likely did not plan my birth, God did! I am not a mistake. No matter how I have perceived myself throughout life, it was God's plan for me to be here before He created the foundations of the world. No demon in hell can thwart the plans of God. They may temporarily succeed at slowing you down by causing you to feel worthless and of no significance, but with God's hand upon you, they can't continue to deceive you with their lies.

Don't be dismayed my friends, although satan is crafty in trying to destroy us, God has the last word. When Jesus died on the cross, he descended into the bowels of hell, disarming the devil of his power to destroy God's creation. He took the keys to death, hell, and the grave. Death has lost its sting because Jesus triumphed over death. We will all die a physical death, however, our spiritual bodies will live on. Where we live through all eternity depends on the choice we make before our physical bodies pass away. If we choose to invite Jesus to come into our lives, we will spend eternity with Him. Otherwise, we will spend eternity in torment and darkness. Never to have any hope of being free from the clutches of satan. Satan only has victory and power over those who give it to him by not receiving Jesus as their Lord and Savior.

Because of the power of the blood Jesus shed on the cross, God's children have the authority to walk in the victory of the cross. The cross and the blood Jesus shed bridged the gap sin causes between us and God. It gave older and tired, and likely unable to see how she could give birth to and raise one more child. She must have felt overwhelmed when she found out she was expecting again. She was then 38, with two-year-old twins. She already had her hands full. She may have had an initial response of shock and confusion, most likely inhibiting her joy. I don't know this to be a fact, however, I "felt" rejected and unloved most of my life. I know she took extreme measures to avoid miscarrying me, resting in bed for several months to avoid losing me.

The earliest lie I believed was part of satan's plan to keep me discouraged throughout my life. It came to me through a "spirit," and this was not the spirit of God. This "spirit" could have come through my mother's emotions when she found out she was expecting. It could have been passed down through a generational curse. It could have come another way also, but regardless of how it came, it was there and caused me to believe the lie, "Nobody loves me."

We are spiritual beings and are born under the curse that Jesus took for us on the cross. God's goodness is stronger than anything the enemy can do to us, but we are all influenced by something. We either walk in blessings or curses. If thoughts of dread, hate, or evil are emotions we express, the spirit of darkness has entered our hearts. Although babies are the most innocent of God's creation, the enemy will do everything in his power to impart his lies to all who will believe them, even in the mother's womb! The earlier he can start coming against us with his deception and lies, the more effective he can

"If we confess our sins, He is faithful and just to forgive us our sins and to cleanse us from all unrighteousness."
1 John 1:9

He will move upon you, cleanse you, and come alive in you to transform your life. You will be a new creation in Christ. The old man will pass away and you will no longer be bound to sin and separation from God. This means the sin and shame that once controlled you, no longer has the power to do so. That old nature dies when you surrender your life to Christ. You will now live, move, and have your being in Him, walking in His fullness and blessings. As you get acquainted with Him through prayer, worship, and reading His Word, you can be delivered from strongholds and addictions that have kept you bound for years.

"Who the Son makes free, is free indeed!"
John 8:36

Walk in your freedom and share the hope that lies within you with others, just as He put in my heart to share with you! This is our calling and our inheritance!

Lord, I ask that You touch every heart reading this message and bless them beyond their ability to understand. Show them Who You are, and as they call upon Your name, fill them to overflowing with Your Spirit and pour Your love out on them in a tangible way. Let them sense Your presence and feel You transforming them as only You can! Turn everything satan has meant for evil in their lives into something that brings You glory. Give them favor as they learn of You and desire to walk in who You called them to be! In Jesus' matchless name, I pray.

"Oh, taste and see that the Lord is good; Blessed is the man who trusts in Him!"

Psalms 34:8

MY TESTIMONY OF HOPE RESTORED

Many years ago before I received Jesus as my Lord and Savior, I was in a terrible pit. I desperately tried to climb out, but I had no strength of my own to do so. Hurting from what life had thrown my way, I didn't believe I could ever have any hope for a life free from pain or sorrow. I felt consumed by rejection and believed nobody loved me or had a reason to. I felt worthless and unworthy of anything good happening in my life, and frankly, I just wanted to die! I truly believed this world, especially my family, would be better off without me. I had lost my ability to trust others, leaving me not knowing where to turn, or how to seek the help I desperately needed.

I was not raised in a Christian home but had a salvation experience that may have been just a "spiritual encounter" as a young teenager. I didn't have anyone to teach me about God, or how to truly know Him. There was no one to encourage me to grow in my relationship with Him. The "enemy" took full advantage of my vulnerability and lured me back into the world.

I lived for years in rebellion and sin, seeking love where real love couldn't be found. When I did find what I thought was love, it only took me deeper into darkness. I became disillusioned with the idea that anyone could "love" the pain away. Everywhere I looked turned into a dead end.

By the time I had been married for ten years with two daughters, I reached the end of myself and knew if something didn't change in my life, I would die. I had been around "religion" and didn't want any part of the hypocrisy I had seen and experienced with it. I didn't know where to turn.

I broke down one day at work and couldn't quit sobbing. I called my sister and told her I needed help. I was broken and desperate to be relieved of this hate I felt for myself and life. She was a member of a local Baptist church I had previously visited with her. She suggested I come that night to mid-week services to speak to her pastor. At this point, I was ready to do almost anything to help me overcome this darkness I was feeling deep inside.

I went to the church and sat through the message. After it was over, my sister asked me to come up to the front and speak to her pastor. I had met him briefly on previous visits, so I was willing to talk to him. She attempted to introduce me, but before she could say my name, he reached his hand out to shake mine, and said, "Well, hey Matcine, it's good to see you again." I was absolutely blown away! It had been a long time since we had last briefly met, and he remembered my name! I had come to truly believe I was invisible, and nobody even saw me, much less remembered me or my name. He had such a heart of love and compassion, that I was immediately ready to hear what he had to say. He prayed for me and suggested I set up counseling with his associate pastor, which I willingly did.

I was counseled and shown the love of God through those He brought into my life. When I cried out for help, Jesus, my True Love, reached out to me! He revealed to me the lies I had believed, so I started walking in the freedom of the Blood Jesus shed on the Cross. Although I still didn't have a full understanding of who I was, I was learning that God loved me and wanted to heal my shattered heart. I received some healing, and was walking in a measure of freedom, but still had not experienced the complete revelation of The Cross.

That is where so many are lost and bound up! The religious shackles and deception of the enemy still have them bound, and they don't truly understand who they are in Christ Jesus! The revelation that the blood He shed on the Cross was for all of our sins: past, present, and future! WE HAVE BEEN FREED BY THE BLOOD OF THE LAMB!

"Hope deferred makes the heart sick, But when the desire comes, it is a tree of life."

Proverbs 13:12

"And they overcame him by the blood of the Lamb and by the word of their testimony, and they did not love their lives to the death."

Revelation 12:11

POSTURE YOUR HEART

Posture your heart to hear My voice, so you know it is I speaking to you. Learn of Me through My Word, and you will recognize My voice. Do not listen to the voice of a stranger, satan, for he will lead you astray. I will lead you on the straight and narrow path. The stranger will take you down the wide path, leading you to eternal separation and death. My ways are higher than your ways, My thoughts are higher than your thoughts. His ways are lower than My ways, and his thoughts lower than My thoughts. My thoughts for you are for peace and not for evil, to give you a future and hope. The stranger's thoughts for you are for torment and not for good, to shatter all of your hope, and to destroy you.

When you call upon Me and pray to Me, I will listen to you. When you seek Me, you will find Me, when you search for Me with all of your heart. When you don't seek Me, you will only hear the voice of the stranger, and you know what his plans are for you. I am always wooing you and will reveal My heart to you if you follow hard after Me. When you don't seek Me with all of your heart, you will not know Me or My heart, but only that of the stranger.

For I AM The Lord your God, there is none other. Don't be deceived into believing you are walking with Me when you do not even know Me. For I know you and the intents of your heart. I am the One who created you. There is nothing you can hide from Me. I know if your heart is pure, or if you're listening to the voice of a stranger. I know your motives and your secrets. Nothing is hidden from Me. Surrender your all to Me today, for the hour of My return is drawing near. I will not tarry much longer, and then it will be too late to call on Me. For I would much rather say to you, "Well done, good and faithful servant," than "Depart from Me, worker of iniquity, I never knew you."

"For I know the thoughts that I think towards you, says the Lord, thoughts of peace and not of evil, to give you a future and a hope."

Jeremiah 29:11

"And you will seek Me and find Me, when you search for Me with all of your heart."

Jeremiah 29:13

"Enter by the narrow gate; for wide is the gate and broad is the way that leads to destruction, and there are many who go in by it. Because narrow is the gate and difficult is the way which leads to life, and there are few who find it."

Matthew 7:13-14

"A perverse heart shall depart from me; I will not know wickedness."

Psalms 101:4

"The thief does not come except to steal, and to kill, and to destroy. I have come that they may have life, and that they may have it more abundantly."

John 10:10

"For as the heavens are higher than the earth, So are My ways higher than your ways, And My thoughts than your thoughts."

Isaiah 55:9

REVEAL ANYTHING IN MY HEART THAT IS NOT OF YOU

Father, I come before You and ask You to expose anything in my heart that is not pleasing to You. Anything, Lord, that keeps me separated in any way from You. Anything that keeps me from hearing Your voice or seeing Your face. I want to be transparent before You, Papa, nothing hidden: no darkness, no idols, or hindrances. Lord, let nothing stop me from fulfilling Your plan and purpose for my life.

King of Glory, fill my heart with Your presence! Fill me up with You, Lord. Let there be no room for anything to hinder me in any way. I surrender all to You and glorify Your Name, Precious Jesus! Pour into me and use me for Your glory!

Give me the boldness to stand before others who are lost and hopeless, provoking me to share the hope of the gospel.

"For I am not ashamed of the gospel of Christ, for it is the power of God to salvation for everyone who believes, for the Jew first and also the Greek."
Romans 1:16

Thank You for never giving up on me, Lord, for giving me another chance to walk in Your love and promises. I love You, Lord, and I will worship You all the days of my life and into all eternity. In Jesus' Name. Amen.
Matcine Pepper

If you are led, please pray this prayer out loud. When we pray out loud, it helps to strengthen us in our spirits, and it also helps the enemy to know that You are washed and covered by the blood of Jesus. That doesn't mean the enemy will stop trying to hinder you, but as you grow stronger in your spiritual walk, he will know that you are a force to be reckoned with and that he is wasting his time trying to bring you down. But just be aware, he never gives up, so keep your armor on always!

(I often reference God as Papa or Daddy. Doing this may not sit well with some, as religious traditions often say, "He is God and should be revered." I feel the same way, however I realize He is a relational God and Father. Therefore, I can freely call Him Daddy or Papa and know there is no condemnation as I am His beloved daughter. He loves when we relate to Him in this personal and intimate way!)

SAVED FROM MY SIN

I was given a job when I was set free,
To share the Light that was shined on me.
I was drowning in darkness, unable to see,
If I trusted the Lord, He would care for me.

God loves us and saves us from all of our sins,
When we open our hearts and welcome Him in.
From the little white lie, you're subject to tell,
Even this small sin can send you to hell.
To the horrible sin of killing someone,
You can still be saved by The Blood of The Son.

So, sin is sin, whether big or small,
He gave us His Son who died for them all.
Just open your heart to invite Him in,
And He will cleanse you of all of your sins.

Matcine Pepper & Mary Alice Miller
March 1994

SUBMIT TO GOD

The scripture says, "Submit yourselves therefore to God, resist the devil, and he will flee from you" (James 4:7). This is a two-step process. The first step is to submit ourselves to God. If we are truly submitted, the devil has to go through Him to get to us. The power of the enemy is no match for God, Who has all power and dominion over us when we are submitted and surrendered to Him.

The enemy knows and so does God. We can't fool either. So, if you are being devoured by the enemy, and your prayers are not making a difference, you may only be fooling yourself.

You might want to re-evaluate your "relationship" with Christ. He has given us ALL power and authority over principalities and powers and rulers of darkness in heavenly places. We are supposed to be the head and not the tail, above and not beneath. We are whole and complete in Him.

Anything less than that may reveal we are not trusting Him with all of our heart, or we may not be walking in the true authority He has given us. Do you truly know Him or just know about Him?

To submit means:

"Accept or yield to a superior force or the authority or will of another person."[1]

To resist means:

1. To take action in opposition to; try to eliminate, reduce, or stop; to oppose.

2. Take action to defeat or thwart (an invading or occupying force).

3. To remain unaltered, undamaged, or unaffected by; withstand.[2]

Do you ever feel your prayers are bouncing off the ceiling? You're saying all the right things, doing your best, being your best, and you feel like God is just out of your reach? Are you submitting to God?

By submitting (surrendering) everything in your life to God, and trusting Him constantly with all of your heart, you are resisting the devil. He no longer has a hold on you and cannot hinder you as you pray. You will see God's hand begin to move as you lay it all at His feet. Trust Him and test His Word.

For most of my "Christian" walk, I struggled with a desire to have a closer relationship with God, as I had seen in others. I never understood the concept of "submitting." I read the Word, went to Church, prayed (when I was desperate and needed Him to help me through a tough situation), worshiped, and even wrote a few poems about how He saved me. But, nothing I was doing was fulfilling that longing in my heart. All of my efforts were nothing more than dead works. I was not submitted to God, therefore He was not on the throne of my heart. I was trying to move the heart of God by my actions and deeds, in a sense, trying to earn His love and blessings, as well as the acceptance of others. All the while, I felt more and more like a misfit. I felt I had no purpose, and questioned whether God even cared about me. I needed to be rescued but didn't know how to cry out to Him.

After going through buying our home, breaking my neck, and then losing my job in the same month, I was ready to give up. However, I had come too far to cave into that temptation. I knew I had greater physical limitations and would not be as helpful to my family or others. But, I still had a heart and desire to encourage others and help those who are downcast, hopeless, and needing courage.

This is where my sister in Christ, and now my Spiritual Mother came into the picture. We casually became acquainted through social media, and soon, I felt a heart connection with her. I felt the love of Jesus coming through her and knew she cared about me and the condition of my soul. My soul was in a pretty dark place at the time, and she was a breath of fresh air for me. She encouraged me in the Lord and helped me to once again feel His hope. She was someone I could trust and share my heart with.

She shared a recorded church service with me and I took the time to watch that 3-hour video. In the end, I was convicted by the Holy Spirit that my heart needed to be cleansed and washed of all I had allowed to come in and darken it. I had to repent and ask God to forgive me for my sin again, as my heart had grown bitter and cold towards Him and others. Allowing this hardness to fill my heart, caused a separation from God. God will not be close to you if you pull away from Him. Sin separates us from Him, and keeps His blessings and grace from working in our lives.

But, His Word says:

"Draw near to God and He will draw near to you. Cleanse your hands, you sinners; and purify your hearts you double-minded."
James 4:8

For the first time in my life, it became clear to me what submitting to God meant. I know now that you have to surrender your will for His will. That means you die to your flesh and selfish desires, and trust God's will and plan for your life. When you fully trust God in your life, you make Him your priority above everything. When you give Him preeminence (make Him first) in your life, He will pour his blessings and favor out on you. Then, as you take your spiritual authority and resist the devil, He will flee from you!

I never imagined I would write a book. While growing in my spiritual walk, and learning to surrender, He started giving me "encouraging words" to post on social media. I began by sharing the Bible App's scripture of the day. As I posted the scripture, I often felt inclined to share something to encourage the reader, along with the scripture. Then as I wrote, instead of a short comment, the next thing I knew, Holy Spirit was downloading things I often didn't have much (if any) knowledge or understanding of. I knew this is only something that God can do.

As I finished writing, I knew I needed to make sure I was hearing God by searching for scriptures to support what I'd written. Occasionally that was a challenge, but I usually found supporting scriptures. If not, I removed anything in the writing I couldn't support with the Word of God.

God will show you His love and favor when you come to the understanding that His plans and purposes will be fulfilled in your life as you submit to Him. Then the enemy will have to flee from you, as you are now submitted to God.

"But without faith it is impossible to please Him, for he who comes to God must believe that He is, and that He is a rewarder of those who diligently seek Him."
Hebrews 11:6

It takes faith in God to be able to submit to Him. Otherwise, He would be forcing you to submit, and God, our Creator, gave us all free will to choose. He will never force His will on us. So, when we submit to Him and His will, He takes it seriously. If we are not truly submitted to Him, we will not obey His Word, or keep our word. If we fail to keep our word and don't repent, then we have proven to Him and ourselves that we never completely surrendered our hearts to God.

We cannot use God as a proverbial pawn, just to get Him to do something we want Him to do, and then wait to call on Him again the next time we need Him. This is manipulation and control: witchcraft. God will not be controlled or manipulated by anyone. He is a Holy and righteous God. If we are truly surrendered to Him, we will submit to Him and acknowledge our need for Him in all things in our lives, not just in the things we pick and choose.

"Let us hold fast the confession of our hope without wavering, for He who promised is faithful."

Hebrews 10:23

"Be sober, be vigilant; because your adversary the devil walks about like a roaring lion, seeking whom he may devour."

1 Peter 5:8

THANK YOU FOR MAKING A WAY OF ESCAPE

Father, Your Word says, *"No temptation has overtaken you except such as is common to man; but God is faithful, who will not allow you to be tempted beyond what you are able, but with the temptation will also make a way of escape, that you may be able to bear it."*
1 Corinthians 10:13

    I thank You, Lord, that throughout my life, especially after I received You as my Savior, You always made a way of escape from the many temptations that came before me. However, You know very well that although You gave me ways to escape the temptations before me, I did not always choose the way of escape.

    My heart was rebellious and I chose to walk in the temptations. I chose the consequences of my choices.

Because You give each person free will, You will never force us to go against our own will. You gave us a conscience and a void within that only You can fill. Our conscience helps us to know, deep within, right from wrong, beginning in our earliest years. But even better than our conscience, once You come into our hearts, You give us Your Holy Spirit to speak to our hearts to tell us when we are stepping out into dangerous waters. He is The Way of escape.

I thank You that even in my rebellion, Your hand has been upon me to guard and protect me from the attempts of the enemy to destroy my life. As I reflect on my life and the many memories, I see how You were there for me in more ways than I ever knew.

As I searched for my identity, I looked everywhere except to You! The enemy of my soul had me blinded to Your truth and kept me distracted just enough to hinder me from hearing Your voice. You always made a way of escape from his temptations, yet I rarely chose Your way.

I somehow thought I would eventually find my significance through "my" efforts. If I kept grabbing at the temptations set before me I would discover my worth. This would surely make me happy, and I would no longer feel hopeless. LIES, LIES, LIES . . . All from the pit of hell.

Satan is a liar and a deceiver: "the father of lies." You cast him out of Heaven because of pride and rebellion, thinking he could become greater than his own Creator, God. He comes only to steal, kill, and destroy all who will believe his deceptions. You sent a Way of Escape, Your Son, Jesus, that we might have life, and have it more abundantly.

Thank You, Father, for sending Your Son to the earth to provide a way of escape to all of those who choose to turn to Him. You make a way where there seems to be no way. Through Jesus, we can walk in the full identity of who You created us to be. As it is made clear, we are all born into sin and need a Savior. When we can see we have a choice in our lives, we can choose to walk in Your forgiveness by receiving You as our Lord and Savior. Then we know our identity is in You, and not in what we perceive others might be saying or thinking about us.

We can then learn about You, Your Son, Your Spirit, the Cross, the Blood, and Your cleansing power to set us free from all that has darkened our hearts. Our true identity is who YOU say we are, and nothing else! You say, I am redeemed, restored, whole, complete, sound not bound, set apart, righteous, holy, more than a conqueror in Christ, loved, accepted not rejected, gifted, full of grace and mercy, filled with the Holy Spirit and power.

You've made me pure and holy, Lord, and I'm humbled in my heart that You chose me before the foundations of the earth to be born for such a time as this. You set me apart for Your good pleasure to be salt and light in the earth. The enemy may have had his time with me, but your unfailing love protected me and kept me from being devoured. He only served to give me a testimony of Your saving grace and to show others how we can all overcome him by the Blood of the Lamb and the word of our testimony.

Your grace is more than sufficient for those who call upon Your name, Lord. Thank You for saving my soul and for helping me to truly know You. I will shout to the earth of Your goodness and mercy all the days of my life. In Jesus' name, Amen.

"Teach me Your way, O Lord, And lead me in a smooth path, because of my enemies."

Psalms 27:11

"Let him know that he who turns a sinner from the error of his way will save a soul from death and cover a multitude of sins."

James 5:20

YOUR BIRTH GAVE ME LIFE AND PURPOSE

Thank You, Father, for Your Son! Before the foundations of the earth, You knew the weakness of man. You created humans to have the ability to choose: free will. You also gave us a sense of right and wrong.

You created us as a spirit in Your image. You made us in many ways so much alike, but in many more ways, so different. We were all designed to live in a body that is very similar to each other, as we were created to each have a torso with 2 arms, 2 legs, 2 hands, 2 feet, 10 fingers, 10 toes, a head with two eyes, two ears, a nose with two nostrils, and a mouth full of teeth to eat with and a tongue to taste with.

We were either made male or female, depending on our sexual organs and whether we have a womb or not, and we all have breasts. You gave us a naval where our umbilical cord was attached to let life flow into us while we developed from an embryo to a fetus, to a baby, while we were in our mothers' wombs. This developmental process was set to last nine months, and the outcome is a new child You imagined before the beginning of time.

You knew us and everything about us before the seed You placed in our earthly father was ever implanted in our mothers' wombs. This very seed determines so much about us that, although it causes us to have the characteristics mentioned above, it includes so much more. It also includes the unique things about us, such as the color of our eyes and our hair, and the tone of our skin. It determines the unique markings on us such as freckles, birthmarks, moles, and whether we have a lot of body hair or only a little.

There are other characteristics, such as our mannerisms and personalities that are more obvious to our parents and family members, as they are passed down from our ancestors in our lineage. These characteristics are deep within our DNA, and they make us unique. They are the traits that carry on the family resemblance. This is why we can usually tell who the parents of children are, especially as the children grow older. We can also compare baby pictures and see the same features of parents and grandparents in their children and grandchildren for generations.

Papa, few people consider the uniqueness You've created in them. Often at a young age, we are made so aware of our shortcomings and our flaws that we become wounded and self-absorbed. Because of the fall of man and sin all around, we often come to believe there is nothing good in us.

Not all, but many have a sense of worthlessness and are filled with self-hate, and lack confidence that our lives have meaning or purpose. We feel empty and hopeless and in desperate need to know our lives have meaning.

This sense of hopelessness comes from the devil, called satan, the enemy of our souls. He is a liar and will deceive all who will listen to and believe him. He is the reason sin even exists. It was satan himself who enticed Adam and Eve to disobey after God said, *"But you must not eat from the tree of the knowledge of good and evil, for when you eat from it you will certainly die" (Genesis 2:17 NIV)*.

Satan convinced Eve that if she ate of the tree, she would be like You, Father. Adam and Eve were created in Your image, so they were already like You. Eve believed him and ate the fruit, and Adam joined her. Their hearts were darkened and filled with shame, so they hid from You. They knew they were naked and did not want You to see. They were separated from You. You told them their seed (all mankind) would be born into sin and separated from You because they chose to walk in disobedience. Therefore, we were born into sin with darkened hearts and a tendency to hear the lies of the enemy.

Thankfully, Father, You also gave the promise of another Seed that You would send to rescue us from our sin and to cleanse us of all unrighteousness. You promised to make a way to redeem us from eternal separation from You.

You came to earth in the form of Your Spirit and overshadowed a young virgin girl named Mary, implanting Your Seed into her womb. You told her she was chosen to carry Your Son, who would take away the sins of the world. He would be called Immanuel, God With Us, and would deliver and set free all who were bound and held in captivity by the enemy. Your Word became flesh and dwelt among us, just as was prophesied at the beginning of time.

All of Your promises either have been or are being fulfilled, even to this very day. We can walk in Your promises for blessings by choosing to receive You as our Lord and Savior, or we can walk in Your promises for curses by choosing to believe the lies of the enemy and not trusting You as Lord. Anyone who chooses to walk according to the desires of his flesh, and not in Your Spirit, is choosing eternal separation and death, by being apart from You.

In Christ, we are made whole and complete, lacking nothing and filled with destiny and purpose. In ourselves, we are powerless and our lives will never have meaning or purpose because we choose to be separated from You. Not choosing is still making a choice, and in the end, it means eternal separation and damnation. Never again will we have the chance to come running to You to receive forgiveness for our sins.

Thank You, Lord, that Your birth gave me, and all who will call on Your name, life and purpose on earth, just as it is in heaven. In Jesus' name, Amen

"Before I formed you in the womb I knew you; Before you were born I sanctified you; I ordained you a prophet to the nations."

Jeremiah 1:5

"I will praise You, for I am fearfully and wonderfully made; Marvelous are Your works, And that my soul knows very well."

Psalms 139:14

"Behold, the virgin shall be with child, and bear a Son, and they shall call His name Immanuel," which is translated, 'God with us'."

Matthew 1:23

"And the Word became flesh and dwelt among us, and we beheld His glory, the glory as of the only begotten of the Father, full of grace and truth."

John 1:14

The Journey To Wholeness

A NEW LIFE HAS BEGUN

"Therefore, if anyone is in Christ, he is a new creation; old things have passed away; behold, all things have become new."

2 Corinthians 5:17

To be in Christ is what makes us Christian. What does "in Christ" mean? As we come to realize how hopeless and empty we are, we need something or someone more wise and loving to steer us through this journey of life. At some point, we come to understand our need for a Savior.

Someone told us about Jesus in some special way: perhaps a friend, a stranger, a pastor, an evangelist, a family member, or you had a wonderful encounter with the Holy Spirit. Or maybe you had an encounter with a spirit of darkness, which made you realize you are destined for an eternity in hell if you don't change the direction you are going. A "spirit of darkness" can come in many forms. Possibly a dream, or a near-death experience. An angel of God could take your spirit to heaven or hell to experience what eternity will be like in either place. There are many ways God can show us that the way we are living our lives will determine our eternal destination.

A couple usually marries because they are in love and want to spend the rest of their lives together. They vow before God and other witnesses to love and serve each other throughout their lives together. They commit their hearts to each other, making each other a priority in their lives. They plan their future and share their love in mutual trust. They laugh and cry together, care for each other in sickness and in health, and prefer their love over any other. They have intimacy, which connects them even greater in the spirit, soul, and body. In essence, they become one as they grow in their lives together.

Sometimes people marry not for love, but for convenience. There is no love between them. A marriage of convenience is contracted for social, political, or economic advantage rather than for mutual affection. It is a union or cooperation formed solely for practical reasons, not for love. Sometimes people can go through the motions of salvation, but they don't experience a transformation. Much like in the marriage of convenience, their heart has not changed and they like being with their Christian friends, but without any commitment of their lives or future to Jesus.

God will woo us with His Spirit, but if we don't come after Him, He will not force us into a relationship with

Him. Again, like that marriage of convenience, we want all of the benefits, without the vital responsibilities of that contract. No love, no commitment, no intimacy, no communication. We get none of the benefits that a genuine committed relationship with Jesus will bring.

Each of us has our own unique experience in this special life-changing transformation. The key word here is transformation! Are you being transformed by the Holy Spirit finding residence in your heart, or did you just change your lifestyle after a religious experience? A religious experience could be seen as more of an emotional experience. You might have been moved by fear of going to hell, causing you to respond to an altar call for salvation. This kind of change requires you to make all of the efforts to be a "good person," but you don't have the power of God through the Holy Spirit working in you to help you change. It's all works of the flesh and not from The Spirit. If there was not a true heart transformation, your life will be empty, and you will struggle hopelessly trying to live up to "God's standards." This is impossible to do on your own without Holy Spirit working in you to help you. God's Word makes it very clear that we become a "New Creation" in Him. When you are transformed, it is evident to you and others that something is different about you. If you were not transformed, that too is evident.

Becoming a Christian is much more than repeating a "sinner's prayer." It is not just about what you say with your mouth, but you must also believe in your heart. When you are facing this life-transforming decision, your heart must be broken over the sin in your life the same way Jesus' heart is broken for us. You must repent for living a life not pleasing to God, and turn away from everything that resembles sin and darkness.

Surrender your all to Jesus. With total surrender, you are admitting you can do nothing in your power to live a life that is pleasing to God. You see your weakness and your need for His strength to help you walk with Jesus in your life. You are humbling yourself and letting go of all pride as you surrender to Him. Now, you no longer walk with both feet in the world, or one in and one out. It's like jumping in a pool. You become submerged in Him!

To be in Christ is like being in the pool. When you first jump or dive in, you are completely submerged and surrounded by water. When you are in Christ, you are completely submerged in Him. If any part of you is not submerged, you risk not walking in His fullness. This doesn't mean you have no hope, but it could mean you have not fully surrendered your life to Him. This is where you ask Him to search your heart and show you anything you need to repent of, thus making Him Lord over your life.

Either you're all in or you're not. This is not a game. We're talking about eternity. It is better if we are either hot (sold out to Him) or cold (still blind to Who He is) than to be lukewarm (1/2 in, 1/2 out). His Word says He will vomit us out of His mouth if we are lukewarm. If you have completely surrendered to Him, you are "in Christ." You are a new creation. Old things have passed away, and all things have been made new.

Surrender is an event, as well as a process. When we realize our need for Jesus to be our Lord and Savior, we surrender our hearts to Him and ask Him to be Lord of our Lives. However, because we live in a fallen world and have temptations constantly before us, we must daily surrender our will to His. We also need to repent if we've done anything that would cause a separation from Him. We ask Him to show us anything that we've done to cause us to be separated from Him, therefore not allowing the enemy a foothold into our lives. As we draw closer to God, He will draw closer to us, and bless us for submitting to His Lordship.

You will now begin to discover who you are in Christ, and what your purpose in life is. Not just your trade or career, but your destiny for which you were created. You will have a hunger for reading the Word and a desire to know His truth and promises. There will be a deeper desire to pray and spend time alone with Him in worship. You will be fulfilled with satisfaction deep within your soul as you learn about and experience the love and the peace of God.

If these are not characteristics in you or you don't long for them, then you may want to question if you truly had a salvation experience. Or, you may have fallen into sin and may need to repent and turn back to Him. Either way, repentance is necessary to be in His grace and to walk in His fullness. So, my question to you is, are you all in or not? Are you hot, cold, or lukewarm? Are you truly "in Christ?"

"Oh, taste and see that the Lord is good; Blessed is the man who trusts in Him!"

Psalms 34:8

"Therefore, laying aside all malice, all deceit, hypocrisy, envy, and all evil speaking, as newborn babes, desire the pure milk of the word, that you may grow thereby, if indeed you have tasted that the Lord is gracious."

I Peter 2:1-3

"But you are a chosen generation, a royal priesthood, a holy nation, His own special people, that you may proclaim the praises of Him who called you out of darkness into His marvelous light; who once were not a people but are now the people of God, who had not obtained mercy but now have obtained mercy."

I Peter 2:9-10

"I know your works, that you are neither cold nor hot. I could wish you were cold or hot. So then, because you are lukewarm, and neither cold nor hot, I will vomit you out of My mouth."

Revelation 3:15-16

"My son, do not despise the chastening of the Lord, Nor detest His correction; For whom the Lord loves He corrects, Just as a father the son in whom he delights."

Proverbs 3:11-12

"As many as I love, I rebuke and chasten. Therefore be zealous and repent. Behold, I stand at the door and knock. If anyone hears My voice and opens the door, I will come into him and dine with him, and he with Me. To him who overcomes I will grant to sit with Me on My throne, as I also overcame and sat down with My Father on His throne."

Revelation 3:19-21

A PRAYER TO ABIDE IN GOD

The following prayer was inspired by Holy Spirit, when reading through my daily Bible devotional. He helped me to reflect on the things He's done and is doing in my life. He brought a very special sister in Christ into my life at a time when I was at one of my lowest points. She became a very dear friend and mentor to me, and because of God's hand on her life and her close relationship with Him, she was used to help me to rise up out of that pit. My mentor holds a very special place in my heart. I'm pretty sure I would not be sitting here typing this, nor would this book even be a thought in my head if it were not for her love for Jesus and her obedience to God's call on her life.

Thank You for never giving up on me, Lord! Thank You for sending Your love to me through my precious mentor and friend. For pouring Your love out on me through someone who freely gives. Because of Your faithfulness to Your Word and Your promises, and because of her love first for You, I was finally able to learn

A Prayer to Abide in God

how to abide in You and let You abide in me. I am now walking in the Joy of my salvation. It is my prayer that others can have a similar experience and know Your love in such a personal way.

Please feel free to make this next part of my prayer personal to you and expect God to move in special ways in your life through it. Although it was personal to me, I feel many will be able to relate:

God, thank You for making a way for me to have a relationship with You. I wondered and wandered for many years searching for what I saw others had, and looking everywhere, except to You. I thought there must be some secret formula I had not discovered. Although I never gave up looking, I became disillusioned, believing the lie that what others had in their relationship with You was not available to me.

Many have been abused, neglected, humiliated, and rejected most of their lives, causing them difficulty having intimacy with anyone, much less their Father in Heaven. They want it but have listened to satan's lies for so long, and do not have faith to believe they are worthy of anyone's love, especially the love of The Father. They have lost their ability to trust. (The intimacy I'm referring to here is not physical, but deep personal heart-felt intimacy, where you can trust and are trusted by someone else, without any fear of betrayal of your trust.)

Use me Lord, and those who walk closely with You, to reach other "misfits" to pour Your love out on. Let them also taste and see that You are good. Set them free from their tormentors and let them walk in the fullness

You have for them. Give them the ability to forgive others who have hurt them. Slam shut in the face of the enemy the doors to cycles of abuse and pain.

May Your plans and purposes be fulfilled in each one of us as we pursue You, and as we abide in You. All relationships take time, care, and effort—so please show us how we can spend intentional time seeking to know You more. In Jesus' name, Amen.

AWAKEN YOU WHO SLUMBER
(A Prophetic Word From The Lord)

Awaken, you who slumber. Harken to My voice. I Am the One who created you, and I tell you, My time for returning is drawing near. The warnings you keep hearing, you need to heed and prepare yourself for. I am the One who established how many days there would be, from the very first day of Creation. I am the One who separated the night from the day. I am the One who set the earth into motion, and I am the One who determines when it's all over.

I warned you in My Word I will soon return for My Bride. I have called you out of darkness into My light so you can prepare yourself for my wedding feast, the Marriage Supper of The Lamb. I warned you to get your lamps ready, to have oil to keep them lit, and to have your wicks trimmed. My return is imminent and is at hand! Your time to prepare is running out, and there is no more time to waste!

Do you know Me? Because if you only know about Me, then I assure you that you will hear, "Depart from Me, I never knew you!" If you never spend time truly seeking Me or getting to know Me, then you will be separated from Me through all eternity.

My heart has longed to spend time with you, My children. I loved you before I even formed the foundations of the earth. Before I ever formed you in your mother's womb, I knew you! I planned your days and established My plans and purposes for your life! You have had many opportunities to be with Me, and you have chosen to go your own way. Just knowing about Me is not enough!

I created you to be one with Me. I sent My Son to die, so that sin could no longer keep us separated. He gave His life for you, making a way for us to be reunited through all eternity. I gave you free will, which gave you the ability to choose, because I will never force anyone to love Me or to walk with Me. I have sent messengers in many ways, yet you still would not turn to Me.

You were created with a void within that only My Spirit could fill, should you only seek after Me and not turn away. I have extended grace to you many times and will even blot out all of your sins because of the precious blood My Son shed for you. I choose to forgive all of your evil ways. All of the many times you chose to walk in sin and not call on My name, I am willing to forgive.

I am a forgiving and merciful God, who will never turn you away. I am coming in the twinkling of an eye; don't wait until it's too late. If you continue to be stiff-necked and hard-hearted, remember you will hear those dreaded words, "Turn away from Me, you evildoer. I never knew you," and you will be cast into outer darkness, where there will be weeping and gnashing of teeth. Your thirst will never be quenched, and the demons who have tormented you in this life will continue to torment you even greater.

So, My children, this is truly a wake-up call. If you are slumbering and going through life as if it's business as usual, you are about to have a rude awakening. Hear My warning, call on My name, and you shall be saved. Turn your back on Me, and I will turn My back on you! My days of grace are quickly coming to an end.

Do I truly know you? I beckon you not to die in your sin. Today is the day of salvation! Call on Jesus, and I will receive you, cleanse you, and make you whole. I will free you from all that has kept you separated from Me, and you will spend the rest of eternity in My presence.

"Not everyone who says to me, 'Lord, Lord,' will enter the kingdom of heaven, but the one who does the will of my Father who is in heaven. On that day many will say to me, 'Lord, Lord, did we not prophesy in your name, and cast out demons in your name, and do many mighty works in your name?' And then will I declare to them, 'I never knew you; depart from me, you workers of lawlessness.'"

Matthew 7:21-23 (ESV)

"For God so loved the world that He gave His only begotten Son. That whosoever believes in Him shall not perish, but have eternal life. For God did not send His Son into the world to condemn the world, but that the world through Him might be saved."

John 3:16-17

"Jesus said to him, "I am the way, the truth, and the life. No one comes to the Father except through Me."

John 14:6

"And if I go and prepare a place for you, I will come again and receive you to Myself; that where I am, there you may be also."

John 14:3

"Let us be glad and rejoice and give Him glory, for the marriage of the Lamb has come, and His wife has made herself ready."

Revelation 19:7

"Watch therefore, for you know neither the day nor the hour in which the Son of Man is coming."

Matthew 25:13

"Oh, taste and see that the Lord is good; Blessed is the man who trusts in Him!"

Psalms 34:8

Do you truly know Me, or just know about Me?

9/24/2022

DON'T CONFORM, BE TRANSFORMED

> *"And do not be conformed to this world, but be transformed by the renewing of your mind, that you may prove what is that good and acceptable and perfect will of God."*
>
> *Romans 12:2*

With all of the craziness and uncertainties in the world today, how is it possible to have even the slightest sense of peace in your heart? The news is filled with violence, hopelessness, despair, sickness and death, mandates from a tyrannical government, political upheaval, wars and rumors of wars, and divisions along ethnic, political, social, and economic lines. Yet, with all this happening, it's possible to have such a sense of peace deep within your heart that, no matter what, you know everything will be all right.

Romans 12:2 says, "Do not be conformed to this world..." So, how can we be a part of this world, yet not be conformed to the world or the things of this world? The rest of the scripture says, "But be transformed by the renewing of your mind, that you may prove what is that good and acceptable and perfect will of God." So, the answer lies within the scripture itself: "Be transformed by the renewing of your mind."

The cares of this world and the pressures of life are going to be with us as long as we are alive and breathing, but how we navigate through them will determine if they toss us back and forth like the waves of the sea, or if we have peace in the midst of the storms.

You can be sure the storms will come. If you've been alive even for 20 years, you already know this is true. If you haphazardly go through life in your abilities, you will be in for a perilous journey. You will be tossed like a rag doll in the hands of a child who has not yet learned how to be gentle in caring for her things. Even if you are well-educated with many degrees, no education can prepare you for the physical and spiritual battles you will face in this journey called life.

How do we renew our minds? It has been proven in psychology that we become like what we focus on. That means our thoughts and lives will reflect those things that have the attention of our hearts, eyes, ears, and minds. The cares of this world will weigh you down and make you feel bewildered and hopeless if you don't have the means to balance the scales to give you hope and peace.

It's Christ in you, the hope of glory (Colossians 1:27).

We are challenged in Romans 12:2 to be transformed by the renewing of our minds. Again, how do we renew our minds? We change our focus from the things of this world to the Word of His Truth. From my personal experience, this is easier said than done.

"On Christ, the Solid Rock, I stand; All other ground is sinking sand. All other ground is sinking sand." The enemy of your soul will do anything in his power to hinder you from being set free from whatever has kept you bound. He knows that as you search God's Word for His truth, you will be set free and no longer be a slave to sin or the things of this world because God's Word is the only real truth. If you search for Him with all of your heart, He will be found. Then His Word comes alive to you and shatters all of the lies of the enemy.

This process can be difficult if we are not pressing into God and asking Him to reveal His truth to us. We must also ask Him to reveal things in us that keep us separated from Him or blind us to His truth. He shows you His truth through the Holy Spirit by impressing a thought into your heart or mind. When He shows you these truths, sincerely turn away from those things; quit sinning and ask Him to forgive you. This is what God's grace is for. In our own power, we cannot just stop sinning. But when we acknowledge our need for His help, and we are sincere about wanting to change, He will give us the grace to do so. Read the Word, pray, worship, listen to a sermon, and enjoy all the surprising ways God will engage with you.

These are all parts of the process of truly knowing

Him. You have to search for Him, and He will be found. Going to church is important, but you can not depend on a pastor or others to help you truly know Him. Knowing Him comes through getting acquainted with Him. It's very personal and intimate. I spent many years looking to others to help me have that personal relationship with Jesus when my greatest hindrances were fear and pride. I had to come to the place where I realized that He is truly all I need. I had to lay down my inhibitions and just trust Him. You can trust Him, too.

As you spend more time in His Word, you are renewing your mind, and being transformed into His image. Then when the devil sends his demons of deception, you will be ready to stand against them. What they say is a lie from the pit of hell. Take your spiritual authority and rebuke them. You have the power to bind them and cast them into the abyss (outer darkness), never to return, in Jesus' Name. This is the power of a Blood-bought Child of the Most High God! Walk in your liberty and the freedom of the Cross. A high price was paid so each of us could be free from the wages of sin and death, even the death of the Cross.

"And you will seek Me and find Me, when you search for Me with all your heart."

Jeremiah 29:13

"For whatever things were written before were written for our learning, that we through the patience and comfort of the Scriptures might have hope."

Romans 15:4

"Ask, and it will be given to you; seek, and you will find; knock, and it will be opened to you."

Matthew 7:7

"But the Helper, the Holy Spirit, whom the Father will send in My name, He will teach you all things, and bring to your remembrance all things that I said to you."

John 14:26

"And you shall know the truth, and the truth shall make you free."

John 8:32

"For I know the thoughts that I think toward you, says the Lord, thoughts of peace and not of evil, to give you a future and a hope."

Jeremiah 29:11

"Hope deferred makes the heart sick, But when the desire comes, it is a tree of life."

Proverbs 13:12

"And I will give you the keys of the kingdom of heaven, and whatever you bind on earth will be bound in heaven, and whatever you loose on earth will be loosed in heaven."

Matthew 16:19

DWELL AND ABIDE

We dwell and abide, as we secretly hide,
While in the secret place, it's in Him we confide.
He is for us, not against us, He is on our side,
He is transforming us into His spotless Bride.

In the secret place, in the shadow of the Almighty,
He protects us and keeps us, He is not flighty.
He is my refuge and my fortress, in Him, I will trust,
There is no other God, He is truly a must.

Surely He shall deliver you from the snare of the fowler,
And from the perilous pestilence, He is our Strong Tower.
With His feathers He covers us, under His wings we hide,
As we surrender to Him, we will dwell and abide.

His truth shall be your shield and your buckler,
And will protect you when you must fight.
You shall not be afraid of the arrow by day,
Nor of the terror that comes by night.

Nor of the pestilence that walks in darkness,
Nor of the destruction that lays waste at noonday.
He will guide us through all we will ever face,
His Word always shows us the Way!

A thousand may fall at your side,
And ten thousand at your right hand.
But it shall not come near your dwelling,
Its foundation is sinking sand.

You will see the reward of the wicked,
As you observe their ways with your eyes.
He shall give His angels charge over you,
As they go to the pit for their lies.

Because the Lord's your dwelling place,
No evil or plague shall befall you.
They will not enter into your space,
Because of what you say and do.

In the angel's hands, they shall bear you up,
Lest you dash your foot upon a stone.
You shall tread upon the lion and cobra,
Because of Jesus, in hell you are known.

The young lion and serpent you shall trample under your feet,
For you were born to win, not live in defeat.
"Because he has set his love upon Me, I will deliver him,"
As My light shines brighter in you,
you'll no longer see things as dim.

I will set him on high because he has known My name.
He searched for Me with all his heart,
and not for fortune and fame.
He shall call upon Me, and I will answer him, too,
And give him directions on what he should do.

I will be with him in times of trouble,
I will deliver and honor him, too.
As he seeks Me with all of his heart,
He will find Me and all that is new.

I will satisfy him with long life,
Because he has chosen Me.
I will show him My salvation,
And open his eyes to see.

So dwell and abide in the Lord Most High,
And watch Me deliver you.
I have many blessings in store ahead,
And much for you to do!

Matcine Pepper
Based on Psalms 91
11/18/2021

ILLUMINATE ALL DARKNESS

God's light will illuminate all darkness so the darkness can't hide. It will be exposed and expelled through the light of His Word.

When we get acquainted with God through reading His Word, His light begins to shine in and through us. Our lights shine very brightly when we are more concerned with how God sees us rather than how others see us.

As we spend time in the Word, we will come to truly know our Heavenly Father. He desires for us to know Him intimately. God wants us to have a deep relationship with Him, so He can reveal His heart and plans to us, and then we can walk in the fullness of His grace and love. We can then be vessels to help illuminate the darkness in others, so they too can be set free.

"You are the light of the world. A city that is set on a hill cannot be hidden."

Matthew 5:14

Besides spending time reading the Word, to grow in our relationship with Him, we can seek Him in prayer—the kind of prayer that asks Him to search our hearts to reveal anything in us, such as sin or deception keeping us separated from Him. As He shows us things we need to surrender to Him, this will help us serve Him and others better. His light will illuminate His truth through us into their lives. Through reading His Word we can draw closer to Him, stirring up a hunger for a greater desire to know Him more.

As you seek Him, if He reveals something, be quick to repent and ask for forgiveness. Anything that causes us to humble ourselves before Him will cause Him to draw closer to us. He is a person, and the power of His Holy Spirit dwells in all of His children. He is the One who encourages and guides us. As we submit to Him, His will becomes apparent. The Holy Spirit is our Comforter, Teacher, Protector, and Helper, the One who leads and guides us as we seek Him. He will gladly show us His will if we truly seek to know Him.

"But the Helper, the Holy Spirit, whom the Father will send in My name, He will teach you all things, and bring to your remembrance all things that I said to you."

John 14:26

When we begin growing in our relationship with Him, He will show us great and mighty things. He will reveal His plan and purpose for our lives, and will even manifest His presence to us as we are in the "secret place" with Him. I often wondered what the "secret place" was until I spent time there. Now that hunger is stirred for Him even more. This is a place of intimacy. Where you can be pure before the Father without any inhibitions, and know His presence is right there with you.

As you grow in your relationship with God, His light shines brighter and brighter in you. This is how we illuminate His light to the world. Being humble and submitted to Him causes us to grow in our Christian walk. It's not in our strength; that is dead works. It's in His strength that we shine His light into the world. As we daily submit our lives to Him, we are surrendering our will to His. We are trusting Him to work His desires and will in us, believing in our hearts that He will be faithful to His Word and promises.

So, rest in Him. Call upon His name, and let Him know how helpless and hopeless you are without Him. He resists the proud but gives grace to the humble. If you want His light to shine brightly through you, you have to give Him your lamp, your heart, so that He can illuminate the darkness for you. Holding back nothing, you will truly know Him as you should.

"But He gives more grace. Therefore He says: "God resists the proud, But gives grace to the humble."
James 4:6

"So we are lying if we say we have fellowship with God but go on living in spiritual darkness; we are not practicing the truth."
1 John 1:6 (NLT)

IN MY WEAKNESS YOU ARE MADE STRONG

Help me Father! As I think about my life in you, Lord, I realize how empty I am without you. How much I need Your guidance and strength each day. Apart from Your Spirit, I am nothing, lacking in every area of my life. I can do nothing worth doing. I am weak and hopeless apart from You. There is no purpose in my life if I try to exist without You for even one second. You are my reason for existence. Why would I think You created me for any reason other than to fulfill Your plan and purpose for my life?

As I grow in my walk with You, Lord, I see how I need You to be on the throne of my heart. When I am separated from You in my heart, I am not walking a surrendered life.

If I try to do anything apart from You, nothing will have true meaning until You are once again glorified in me.

My will is shallow, and self-seeking, leading to spiritual and eternal death. Your will is purposeful, and fulfilling, leading to spiritual and eternal life. Your will is Your plan for my life and for the lives of all who trust and follow You. When our hearts long to do Your will, our desire is to please You in all we say and do. We can only please You as we seek to know You and Your will for our lives. Out of our desire to know You, a hunger for Your Word grows. To know You is to know Your Word. You are the Word and the only true Living God.

"Your Word is alive and powerful, and sharper than any two-edged sword, piercing even to the division of soul and spirit, and of joints and marrow, and is a discerner of the thoughts and intents of the heart."
Hebrews 4:12

Purify my heart, O God, make me holy as You are Holy! If anything is blinding or deceiving me in any way, open my eyes to see Your truth. Let me walk in Your perfect will for my life. Cleanse me of all unrighteousness, and help me surrender daily to You! Help me crucify my flesh and no longer live for myself, keeping my life pleasing to You! Give me a heart of repentance so I can come daily before You with a clean and pure heart.

Without Your Spirit dwelling in me, there is no way I could have these desires, Lord. Thank You, Holy Spirit, for living in me and keeping me hungry for the things of God. Thank You that You will never leave me nor forsake me. As long as I am humble before You, I will always walk according to the way You designed me. You in me and I in You. Never lacking and always fulfilling Your perfect plan for my life. May I always be weak so that You are made strong in me! In Jesus' precious name! Amen.

And He said to me, "My grace is sufficient for you, for My strength is made perfect in weakness." Therefore most gladly I will rather boast in my infirmities, that the power of Christ may rest upon me.

2 Corinthians 12:9

OBEDIENCE IS BETTER THAN SACRIFICE

Lord, with all that is in me, I surrender my heart to You. You called me out of darkness into Your marvelous light. You gave Your life for me, so what gives me any right to withhold anything from You? If I withhold from You, I am not fully surrendered to Your will for my life.

There have been parts of my heart I have not released to You for fear of the pain of loss—I would not know how to go forward with that pain in my heart. Therefore, I have not been obedient to what I have sensed You calling me to do. Your Word says, "To obey is better than sacrifice," (1 Samuel 15:22) and although there is almost always a sacrifice involved when You call us to do something, You honor our faithfulness to You through our obedience.

Because of Jesus' obedience to what You sent Him to do, to surrender (sacrifice) His life on the cross, I am able to call on Your name right now. Because of His obedience to lay His life down, to die for all mankind, I and all who receive Him as their Lord and Savior, have the right to come before You as a Blood-bought Child of The Most High God. Only through Your Son can we come to You.

When we surrender our all to You, it shows our faith and trust in You, and You alone. It shows we can be trusted with what You have in store for us. He Who is faithful with little will also be faithful with much. (Luke 16:10) However, when we are not completely surrendered to You, we have a divided heart. When our hearts are divided, can You trust us with what You want us to do? We are only fooling ourselves if we think we can straddle the fence and still please You.

Forgive me, Father, for withholding from You. By doing so I have been showing my lack of trust in You and Your plans for my life. I repent and lay all of my apprehensions down at your altar. Everything that has become an idol in my life and has taken precedence over You, I lay before You. I know these things may not all be inherently bad, but allowing them to become a greater focus in my life than You, has been my snare.

Forgive me for my disobedience and help me to go forward in my walk, fully trusting that You are all I need in my life to keep and sustain me. Nothing and no one is of more value than You. Please help me to stay focused on You so that I do not put any more gods before You ever again. In Jesus' Precious name, I pray, amen!

"But you are a chosen generation, a royal priesthood, a holy nation, His own special people, that you may proclaim the praises of Him who called you out of darkness into His marvelous light;"

I Peter 2:9

"So Samuel said: "Has the Lord as great delight in burnt offerings and sacrifices, As in obeying the voice of the Lord? Behold, to obey is better than sacrifice, And to heed than the fat of rams. For rebellion is as the sin of witchcraft, And stubbornness is as iniquity and idolatry. Because you have rejected the word of the Lord, He also has rejected you from being king."

I Samuel 15:22-23

"And being found in appearance as a man, He humbled Himself and became obedient to the point of death, even the death of the cross."

Philippians 2:8

"All things are lawful for me, but all things are not helpful. All things are lawful for me, but I will not be brought under the power of any."

1 Corinthians 6:12

THE LORD OF THE RING

I once worked in a hospital as a clerk. Young and married with two children, my husband and I struggled to make ends meet. Occasionally, a jewelry salesman came into the hospital, selling rings and other merchandise. He interested me because I had lost the main stone in my engagement ring a couple of years earlier. I found a simple engagement ring in his inventory that I really liked. I wanted to have the ring on my finger to signify I was committed to the man I loved.

I had the ring checked out by a jeweler friend of mine. He verified that it was a great bargain. The only problem was we would have to miss paying a couple of bills to pay for the ring.

My kind husband agreed that I should buy the ring because I wanted it so badly. But then I was prompted by the Holy Spirit to pray first. I prayed, knowing I would have to wait for an answer. Then, I happened to glance at an inspirational flip calendar on my desk. The scripture that day was Proverbs 3:5-6: "Trust in the Lord with all of your heart, And lean not on your own understanding; In all your ways acknowledge Him, And He shall direct your paths." At that point, I knew I needed to wait on the Lord for a ring.

I had possibly seen these scriptures before, but not as an answer to prayer! Since accepting Jesus as my Savior, I had never really stepped out in faith to trust Him like this.

A couple of weeks passed. My Aunt Matcine, for whom I was named, was admitted for rehab in my hospital. She was sick and likely dying of cancer. It was so special that she was now in town and close to us, allowing my family and me to spend some precious time with her.

One Sunday when I walked into her room to visit, she was not there. I was shocked, as I had not heard she was being discharged or moved. Then I found out she had taken a turn for the worse and was now in intensive care. I called my mother, and we met in the ICU waiting room. I went in to see my aunt for a few minutes and could tell her time was short. She could barely talk but kept trying to tell me something. All I could understand was "namesake." I told her, "Yes, I'm your namesake and honored to be so," expressing how much I loved her. Then I had to leave.

As I went back and shared this with my mom, I explained I could only understand "namesake." Mom said, "Oh, I know what she was trying to say to you. She told me several months ago that she has a ring she wants you to have when she passes. It is a solitaire diamond with ten small diamonds clustered around it."

Oh my! I could not believe what I was hearing. God knew the desire of my heart! Now, some 30 years later, I see it was a gift from my Bridegroom to show me He was calling me His, and soon He will return to receive me as His bride. Now I am wrecked. What a loving and generous Father we have. What an honor to have an aunt who blessed me with something so special, to remind me of her love, and the love of My Heavenly Father.

I could have bought the other ring and would still have received Aunt Matcine's, but waiting on God, He fulfilled my heart's desire without adding stress to our finances and marriage. The intangible value of Aunt Matcine's ring was far greater than any other ring I could have given myself. It is always a wonderful and constant reminder of my Father's love for me!

The special things He has in store for us are always better than what we can do on our own. He's such a good, good God! Thank You, Father, for loving and caring for us, as we trust in You with all of our hearts.

"Trust in the Lord with all of your heart, And lean not on your own understanding; In all your ways acknowledge Him, And He shall direct your paths."
Proverbs 3:5-6

"Delight yourself also in the Lord, And He shall give you the desires of your heart."
Psalms 37:4

WAIT UPON THE LORD

Wait upon the Lord
In all that you do,
When you surrender to Him
He will take care of you.

As we abide in Him
Through each night and day,
He will answer our prayers
And lead us His way.

He gave us His best
When He sent us His Son,
As He died on the cross
For everyone.

Without having Jesus
In your heart deep inside,
There is no way
That one can abide.

There is much
He has for us to do,
But, without knowing Him,
Who has a clue?

We must know more
Than just who He is,
Just knowing about Him
Doesn't make us His.

Do you truly know Him,
What His heart is for you?
Or just know about Him,
With really no clue?

To know Him is to love Him,
And to surrender your all.
Only knowing about Him,
Could cause you to fall.

As you grow in your walk
Each day of your life,
He's transforming you from
His bride to His wife.

The two become one
As you worship and pray.
As you read His Word
He's known more each day.

As you walk and talk with Him,
You're learning to abide.
He will make you complete,
As His spotless bride.

Today is the day
To call on His name,
He will receive you with love
And remove all your shame.

Wait upon the Lord
in all that you do,
When you surrender to Him
He will take care of you.

Matcine Pepper
12/19/2022

YOUR LOVE KNOWS NO BOUNDS

Father, I thank You for loving me, even though You know everything about me. You know the good, the bad, my ups and downs, my strengths, my weaknesses, my faults, and my virtues. With all You know about me, You still love me; please Lord, help me to have this same love for others.

I have always felt the bad in me outweighs the good. The bad made me loathe who I was. Yet it is the loathing that finally helped me see my need for a strength besides my own to enable me to continue down the path of life!

What I knew and believed about myself only led to more destruction and hopelessness, until I finally came to a point where I had to believe there must be more to life than this. I had to reach the end of myself and stop trying to live this life on my own. I had to cry out to You and acknowledge I am helpless and hopeless without You in my life.

Now, I see it was Your Spirit wooing me to You. It's Your agape (unconditional) love for me and all mankind that leads us to repentance. You made us need You so our lives can glorify You. Our lives only have meaning and purpose when You are on the throne of our hearts (when we have surrendered our lives to You). There is nothing or no one who can fill the God-given void within us but You! In You, we live, and move, and have our being. Apart from You our lives will never shine or offer any hope to others. You designed us in such a wonderful way, Father, and I thank You for making a way where there seemed to be no way.

We are all on the road to destruction when we try to live our lives in the flesh, or according to the ways and standards of the world. You use our circumstances and the hopelessness they bring, then You often use others who are walking with You to help guide us to You. You made us need You, and You'll always do whatever it takes to cause us to come running to You. You are the reason we're alive, and why we can live eternally if we choose to walk with You.

Help me, Lord, to shine Your light brightly in this earth, so others will know there surely is a God in Heaven. Oh, Lord of the universe, be magnified in my life and use me for Your glory. "May the words of my mouth and the meditations of my heart be *ever so* pleasing in Your sight, Oh God, my strength and my Redeemer" (Psalms 19:14; *emphasis mine*).

Help me to show others they can have a truly intimate relationship with their Father in Heaven. You created them before the beginning of time, know everything about them, and still love them. Let that same love radiate out of every fiber of my being as I go forth each day, in Jesus' Mighty Name! Amen

"Oh, taste and see that the Lord is good; Blessed is the man who trusts in Him!"

Psalms 34:8

Take a moment now to look up and read Acts 17:24-31.

Salvation, Deliverance, and Freedom

A LIGHT WILL SHINE

Do you see God's light shining? It is there, but if all you see is darkness, then you might want to question, Do I truly know Him? Is Jesus the Lord of my life, or just someone I know about in my head? Has my heart changed? Did I have a real salvation experience?

My friend, this is something we need to have settled deep within our hearts. The hour of Jesus' return for His spotless bride is very near. It could be too late if you postpone confirming you are a Child of the King. What have you got to lose? Everything! What have you got to gain? Everything!

If you are uncertain that you are ready to meet Jesus, ask Him to show you. Ask Him to speak to your heart and to give assurance that you are His and He is yours. If you are still unsettled, then ask Him to come into your heart. To save your soul. To set you free and to forgive you of your sin, all sin: past, present, and future.

Repent, receive His forgiveness, and know deep inside with His help, you will no longer desire to walk in willful sin. If you do stumble and sin, ask Him to forgive you (as often as necessary), to fill you with His Spirit, and give you a hunger for His Word. Renew your mind with His Word, so you no longer sin due to old habits, as you seek daily to learn and grow in Him. Ask Him to put His love for others in your heart, and a desire to share His love with lost and hurting souls. They are hopeless and dying in their sin—like you once were.

Surrender to Him all you are and all you have. You will never give up more than you will gain. What the world has to offer does not compare to what a life in Christ can give you.

He created us in His image, yet we're each unique in our way. We all have a specific purpose for being born, but until we surrender to Him, we will never fully walk in our God-given purpose. You were born for such a time as this! Don't let another moment go by without knowing your eternal destiny is settled, by making Him the Lord of your life. This is the most important decision you will ever make in your life. He died for you, so you can truly live for Him.

"The people who walked in darkness Have seen a great light; Those who dwelt in the land of the shadow of death, Upon them a light has shined."
Isaiah 9:2

"Ask, and it will be given to you; seek, and you will find; knock, and it will be opened to you."
Matthew 7:7

*"But he who sins against Me wrongs his own soul;
All those who hate Me love death."*
Proverbs 8:36

"Search me, O God, and know my heart; Try me, and know my anxieties; And see if there be any wicked way in me, And lead me in the way everlasting."
Psalms 139:23-24

"Whoever has been born of God does not sin, for His seed remains in him; and he cannot sin, because he has been born of God."
1 John 3:9

DO YOU KNOW THE RESURRECTION

Have you been resurrected by The Resurrection? There is a life you know nothing about if you haven't been raised from the dead. Do you know you can be dead and still breathe? There are people all around you, and maybe even you, who are dead in spirit, yet they walk around in their physical bodies.

Because of Lucifer's (satan's) disobedience, rebellion, and pride, before the beginning of Creation, we were destined to be separated from God. God already knew that satan would deceive Adam and Eve by making them believe they could become as smart as God. God is Holy, and sin cannot be in His presence. A longing and a plan were in God's heart to defeat sin and death to reunite His family. At the coming together of the ages, God sent His Son by His Spirit in the form of a seed which the Holy Spirit implanted in the womb of a young virgin: Mary. He was born Jesus, the Son of God, who became human flesh and lived among us. He walked on the

Earth and was tempted in all ways as we have been, yet without sin. He came to deliver us from our fallen nature so we could be reunited with God.

Jesus was looked upon with contempt by the religious leaders, so they chose to charge Him for crimes he did not commit. They whipped Him with whips filled with barbs and stones, ripping through His flesh. They condemned Him to death by crucifixion—hanging on a cross, the most agonizing way anyone could die. He was our sacrifice according to the religious laws of those days. He became the pure spotless Lamb who died in our place to save us from eternal damnation.

He died a painful death and was buried in a borrowed tomb. On the third day, He came alive again, walking out of the tomb that had been barricaded against His escape, leaving us a symbol of what it is to be born again. He walked the earth for 40 more days and ascended into Heaven to sit at the right hand of the Father, God, our Creator. Jesus is the Bridegroom waiting to return for all who have received Him as their Lord and Savior, His Church, His spotless bride, to take them with Him into eternity.

The life I'm referring to is a life beyond what the "natural mind" can imagine. It's not something farfetched; it's more real than the air you breathe. It's a life of peace and of purpose. It's a life in Christ, the Creator of all heaven and earth. It's what you have been searching for since you were born.

He created you with a need for Him and a conscience so you can know right from wrong. You might not have realized it, but God created you for purpose and significance, something you have searched for your entire life. Nothing else will ever satisfy like Jesus! Jesus is the Way, the Truth, and the Life, no one comes to the Father except by Him (John 14:6).

We are knocking on the door of eternity, my friends. That means He will return very soon. We are eternal souls who will spend forever in either Heaven or hell. The choice is ours. God is no respecter of persons; we were all given free will, having the ability to make our own choices. We are not created as robots, but are unique, with the ability to choose.

We can choose to make good decisions or bad. If we choose to reject Jesus as our Lord and Savior (a bad decision), we have chosen eternal damnation. That means a life forever separated from Him, His love, peace, joy, hope, healing, and all His promises—choosing instead, to spend eternity in the "Lake of Fire" with your adversary, satan. "Satan, the thief, only comes to steal, kill, and destroy. But, Jesus came that we can have life, and have it more abundantly" (John 10:10).

There is a battle for our souls, but because of the blood of Jesus shed on the Cross, we get to choose life or death. By not choosing, you are still making a choice to be eternally separated from the One who loves and died for you. You are choosing instead to spend eternity in hell, where there will be weeping and gnashing of teeth, with satan, the one who was cast out of Heaven for pride and rebellion against God (Matthew 8:12).

By choosing Jesus (a good decision), when you die,

you will instantly be in His presence for eternity. You will walk the streets of gold, and you will have a mansion built just for you (Revelation 21:21, John 14:2). You will be with others who have chosen God, both before and after you. Heaven is a real place, and so is hell. The choice is truly yours.

One more thing, if you said a "sinners prayer" with no change or transformation, you are paving your way straight to hell. Don't let the devil fool you.

Giving your life to Christ means being filled with His righteousness, peace, and joy. Dying to your selfish desires, embracing His will, and His plans for you. You may see it as having to give things up, but you are gaining so much more! God gives the peace your heart longs for. Only He can fulfill your purpose and make your life satisfying, bringing Him glory.

Please don't let the enemy of your soul rob you any longer. Ask God to forgive you and show you how to walk, complete in Him! It is in Him we live, and move, and have our being (Acts 17:28). Choose Christ and know this is the best decision you will ever make in your life (past, present, and future). Forever, you will live and not die.

"But God, who is rich in mercy, because of His great love with which He loved us, even when we were dead in trespasses, made us alive together with Christ (by grace you have been saved)."

Ephesians 2:4-5

Jesus said to her, "I am the resurrection and the life. He who believes in Me, though he may die, he shall live. And whoever lives and believes in Me shall never die. Do you believe this?"

John 11:25-26

DON'T LET YOUR HEART BE TROUBLED

Who can deny we live in troubled times? There has never been a time in our lives that evil has been so rampant: sickness and disease everywhere, plagues, pestilence, and pandemics, wars and rumors of wars, perversion of everything that can be perverted, killing of innocent lives, good being called evil and evil being called good.

People, especially God's people, are being tested and stretched on all sides. The Earth is shaking and rumbling with earthquakes and volcanoes. The atmosphere is full of all sorts of activity such as floods, snow storms in places that rarely ever see snow, historic-sized hail, sinkholes opening up and swallowing everything nearby, fires raging, burning anything around, and so many more strange phenomena.

Governments are corrupt and deceiving others for their own selfish and evil gain. News media is out of control, not reporting the news as it happens, but following an agenda that will benefit certain evil schemers. There is so much more, but I think you get the picture.

According to God's Word, The Bible, there are seasons for all things. We just didn't know all of these seasons would converge at the same time.

"To everything there is a season, A time to every purpose under heaven: A time to be born, And a time to die; A time to plant, And a time to pluck what is planted; A time to kill, And a time to heal; A time to break down, And a time to build up; A time to weep, And a time to laugh; A time to mourn, And a time to dance; A time to cast away stones, And a time to gather stones; A time to embrace, And a time to refrain from embracing; A time to gain, And a time to lose; A time to keep, and a time to throw away; A time to tear, And a time to sew; A time to keep silence, And a time to speak; A time to love, And a time to hate; A time of war, And a time of peace."

Ecclesiastes 3:1-8

But, be encouraged my dear friends, the Word says more! With God, there is always hope! He made a way of escape through His Son, Jesus, for all who call on His Wonderful Name. He says:

"Let not your heart be troubled; you believe in God, believe also in Me. In My Father's house are many

mansions; if it were not so, I would have told you. I go to prepare a place for you. And if I go and prepare a place for you, I will come again and receive you to Myself; that where I am, there you may be also. And where I go you know, and the way you know."

John 14:1-4

There is hope in Christ and in Him alone. There is no other who can rescue you from the torment and disasters to come. We are living in the last days, my friends. I implore you, if you don't know Jesus Christ as your Lord and Savior, today is the day of Salvation. We truly don't know what tomorrow will bring.

With the uncertainty of the times we're living in, there is one thing we can be certain of: God has made a way in the hard places for all who call upon the name of Jesus. He sent His Son as a living sacrifice for our sins, to die an unbearably painful death so we could have Jesus as our connection to the Father. He is the only way, and there is no other. If you've never called upon His Name, or if you've never really made Him Lord of your life by surrendering everything to Him, please don't wait another second. We are not guaranteed our next breath. Ask Him into your heart.

"Jesus said to him, "I am The Way, The Truth, and The Life. No one comes to The Father except through Me."

John 14:6

Repent from all sin: Admit you are a sinner, and never look back to those things that kept you separated from God. Ask Him to come into your heart, to fill you with His Spirit, and to make you whole. He is waiting to receive you into His arms and His Kingdom.

You will come out of hopelessness and despair into His marvelous light. Trust God! Once you surrender to Him, your life will never be the same. He has a plan and purpose for each of us, but until you become a child of the Most High God, you will never know your full purpose in this life.

I pray you don't put off making this life-changing, eternal decision. You can't even imagine the peace that will flood your soul as you turn your eyes upon Jesus. He is waiting to receive you into His arms with much to give you.

"Oh, taste and see that the Lord is good; Blessed is the man who trusts in Him!"

Psalms 34:8

If you've made this decision and have questions, please connect with a believer in Christ Jesus or a Bible-preaching Spirit-filled church, or search the Bible! There are many Bible apps you can add to your phone, tablet, iPad, or computer. Pray and ask the Holy Spirit to guide you to the answers you are looking for. God's Word says: "So I say to you: Ask and it will be given to you; seek and you will find; knock and the door will be opened to you" (Luke 11:9). If you've had a heart conversion and are seeking answers from God, He will not leave you wanting. He says, "And you will seek Me and find Me, when you search for Me with all your heart" (Jeremiah 29:13).

"For I, the Lord your God, will hold your right hand, saying to you, 'Fear not, I will help you.'"

Isaiah 41:13

"Then the Lord said to him, "Peace be with you; do not fear, you shall not die."

Judges 6:23

"Fear not, for I am with you; Be not dismayed, for I am your God. I will strengthen you, Yes, I will help you, I will uphold you with my righteous right hand."

Isaiah 41:10

"The Lord bless you and keep you; The Lord make His face shine upon you, and be gracious to you; The Lord lift up His countenance upon you, and give you peace."

Numbers 6:24-26

"But from there you will seek the Lord your God, and you will find Him if you seek Him with all of your heart and all of your soul."

Deuteronomy 4:29

HE WHO PROMISED IS FAITHFUL

No matter what God promises, we have the assurance of knowing He will fulfill His promises. Whether they are promises of hope or judgment, He is a just God and never reneges on what He says. Our God, the God of the Heavens and the Earth, Creator of the Universe, is faithful and true to His Word.

So, if you want to walk in His promises of hope, you must make sure you know the God of Hope, and not just about Him. Merely knowing about Him indicates that you don't have His truth in your heart. If you did, you would already know you have all of His promises for hope and a future. You wouldn't be wavering and wondering if your salvation is secure. You would know that you know, if your next breath is your last, you would have the assurance of instantly being in His presence.

This assurance only comes as you have intimate fellowship or communion with the Father. If you seek Him with all of your heart daily, talk to Him in prayer always, walk in humility with a heart sorry for your sin; if you repent and worship Him; if you get acquainted with Him by renewing your mind through reading the Word, and share the hope within you by testifying of His goodness and faithfulness, you can then stand before Him with the assurance that You are His child. All of His promises for hope are Yes and Amen for you.

The fear of His wrath and judgment will not loom over you because you have chosen to surrender your all. You have chosen to deny the appetites of your flesh as you take up your cross and follow Him! You know His voice and no longer hear or listen to the voice of the devil. You have learned to, submit to God and resist the devil, therefore, causing him to flee (James 4:7).

When you know who you are and Whose you are, you will no longer flounder in the sea of doubt, wondering if your salvation is secure in Christ. It is secure because of the blood Jesus shed on the cross at Calvary. Without Him shedding His blood and dying for our sins, we would all be without hope and would perish in our sins, spending eternity separated from God.

If you do not choose to walk in His promises, you are automatically choosing to walk in His judgment. No matter how good a person you are, or think you are, without purposefully choosing to accept Jesus as your Lord and Savior, without also repenting of your sin—"for all have sinned and fallen short of the glory of God" (Romans 3:23)—you can be certain you will have no part in the blessings of God when you breathe your last breath.

You will not enter into His presence, and the only reason you will see Him is to be judged for your sin. You will have to answer for every sin committed and idle word spoken. You'll be punished accordingly. You will be cast into outer darkness, where there will be weeping and gnashing of teeth. Your soul will be constantly tormented with fire, and you will have an unquenchable thirst, as there will be no water to satisfy you. Demon spirits will constantly torment you, along with all the other souls they've kept blinded from the truth. Pride and rebellion opened the door for their entry into your life. Receiving Jesus as your Savior and serving Him is the only thing that will close that door.

Nobody was meant to spend eternity in hell. Hell was created for satan and the fallen angels who rebelled against God for the sin of pride. Please, Father, I ask for Your mercy. Open blind eyes and deaf ears. Show them Your heart for all mankind, and cause them to turn from their wicked ways, in Jesus' name, Amen!

Please go on a journey through the Scriptures and read the referenced verses below to hear the heart of God as He supports the word He has given me for you.

Hebrews 10:23, 26-27, 30-31, 36
1 John 1:5-10
Romans 3:23
2 Corinthians 5:9-10
Matthew 25:30

HOLY SPIRIT, HELP THOSE WHO ARE HURTING LEARN HOW TO TRUST YOU

Oh, Father, my heart is aching right now for those who have been wounded through betrayal, rejection, neglect, violation, abuse, lies, and deceit. They have been devalued and dishonored by those who were supposed to love and care for them—family and loved ones who should give love, yet instead have taken all they can and then some. Instead of family and loved ones being places of safety, they have become places of trauma and loss. Instead of learning how to grow up to feel safe and secure, they have learned how to hide their pain by closing their hearts and spirits to You and anyone You're working through.

Their ability to trust is broken, and they don't even know it. They appear strong, capable of living well in their strength, and not depending on You for strength. They are deceived, as the enemy has blinded them. Although they may say they know You, their hearts are far from You. They have a form of godliness, but deny Your power to work in them because their faith has been shaken by the greed and cruelty of others.

Because their ability to trust is broken, they cry out to You, yet they don't receive You. Their guard is up. They do not know how to allow You or anyone else close to their hearts for fear of more pain and betrayal. They are bound in fear, therefore they build emotional distance from You and others. They continue living in fear of love, erecting a fortress around themselves for protection. They attempt to protect themselves from the very One Who can save and restore to them all that the enemy has stolen.

Oh, Papa, Creator of all the heavens and earth, Who Was, Who Is, and Who Is To Come; Lord of all, Holy is Your name! Your Spirit dwells within us to quicken our mortal bodies. Unlock the chains from Your people. Set them free and make them whole and complete in You, Lord.

Your Word says You sent Your Son to deliver the captive, to set us free from sin and death. Set free those who are bound. Pour out Your love through the Holy Spirit to unlock the shackles that keep them bound up. Pour Your love and mercy out on them causing them to see Your Mighty Hand move in their hearts.

Put them in a safe place in You, separating them from those who refuse to acknowledge You. Let them experience true LOVE as You envelop them in Your pure agape Love. A love beyond anything man is capable of giving. Take away the stony hearts and replace them with hearts of flesh, allowing You to mold and make them into the beautiful people You always intended them to be.

Move each one into the destiny You created for them, strengthening them so they will resist the enemy's deception again. Use them in the lives of those who need healing, even as You heal and restore them. Take everything satan meant for evil in their lives and use it all for Your glory. You have the last Word, Lord. Show them You truly have defeated death, hell, and the grave, and they no longer have the power to destroy their lives. In Jesus' precious name, I pray! Amen, and amen.

LORD, PLEASE OPEN MY EYES

Dear Lord,
Please open my eyes that I might see
All of the things that hinder me,
From walking in Your grace and love,
From setting my sight on things above.

There are physical things I see each day,
They seem to be what's in my way.
They're only just the manifestations,
Of the spiritual bondage that comes from satan.

Please open my eyes in a greater way,
So I am no longer satan's prey.
Make me aware of his devices,
Let me not be fooled by his entices.

Not only myself do I pray this for,
But help my family walk through Your door.
Let all other doors that have been opened,
Be shut forever. Your Word's been spoken.

Your Word says, "The truth shall set us free."
Let our lives reflect Your victory.
Help us be a witness and example to all,
Of Your grace and Your mercy to those who call.

Thank You Lord, for helping me see,
In You I have the victory.
You paid the price on that dreadful day,
For me to be free, You are The Way.
Amen

Matcine Pepper
10/5/1998

NEW HOME AND JOB LOSS TESTIMONY

No matter what you're going through, whatever curveballs life throws your way, if you know Who holds the future, then you don't have to worry about what the future holds. God is in control from the throne, and whatever happens, trust His plan is being fulfilled in your life. Even if you don't understand it all, He knows best and has a better plan than you or I could ever come up with.

There was a season not long ago when many changes were happening in my life. Some seemed good, some not so good, but what we perceive as good or bad may be a false perception. In less than a month, two chapters of my life closed. The first was completing the move from the house we rented for 13 years. It took a whole month for us to get out. Packing, purging, selling, cleaning, and moving was one of the hardest things we had encountered in a long time. Without some very special family members and friends, we never would have gotten through this. You know who you are, and so does God! I pray God will bless each of you in mighty ways.

We were tired and trying to recuperate from the move, taking it one day at a time. We were no longer spring chickens, so bouncing back from the energy we spent on moving was not as easy as it once was, but God's grace was sufficient to help us through. We can do all things through Christ, who strengthens us (Philippians 4:13).

Then on April 5, 2019, what I thought would be a "normal" work day turned out to be anything but "normal." My job of eight-and-a-half years came to an end. The company I worked for had experienced a reduction in business over the past couple of years and decided to reduce the workforce some more. This was the second layoff in as many months, and my position was eliminated. Five full-time and a few temporary personnel were let go that day. I was blindsided and in shock. I had made many great connections and friends with a wonderful group of people, and felt like I lost part of my family that day. It was hard and I still miss everyone so much. I appreciated all the prayers on our behalf as my friends and I adjusted to no longer working together.

When God closes one door, He will open others. God sees the whole picture, while we only see in part. Our perceptions can mislead us, causing us to worry about things we have no need to be concerned about. When we worry, in essence, we're saying, that God is not big enough to take care of us or our needs. He didn't put us here to stress and worry about things, but to live for Him, being filled with His joy and peace—reflecting His light brightly so others too can walk in His peace and joy. His plans are perfect, and He will never disappoint or let us down. I am learning to rest in Him and wait for His direction in my life. He had a reason for shutting the door on this chapter, and I trust He will lead me where He wants me to go.

As I reflect on this time not so long ago, I can now see more of God's purpose for allowing things to happen as they did. The season I was in had to change so God could move me into His ultimate purpose for creating me. He gave me the gift to write, and to share His heart. The time has come for what He has prepared me for—to share the messages He has inspired me to write. More chapters to my story are sure to come, as I seek His will and plan for my life. As I surrender my will to His, He will open new doors of opportunity for me in the days ahead. He is no respecter of persons, and what He has done for me, He will do for you as you draw closer to Him in your Journey to truly know Him.

READY OR NOT, HE'S COMING SOON

There are many who are figuratively playing with fire by living their lives as if they have all the time in the world to do anything they choose. They don't realize, that unless they receive Jesus as their Lord and Savior, they literally will soon be burning in the lake of fire throughout all eternity.

There are also those who may have said a "sinner's prayer" at some point in their lives, but they were never transformed, therefore they were never truly saved. Seeing themselves as good and unable to understand they are living a lie, they have been hoodwinked by the master deceiver, the devil. The Bible says,

"The way of a fool is right in his own eyes. But he who heeds counsel is wise."

Proverbs 12:15

So many things are happening in the world today. If you open your eyes and heart, maybe you will see the seriousness of what God has placed in my heart, from His heart.

God has brought a separation between those who are walking in darkness, and those who are walking in His forgiveness. There are telltale signs that distinguish the two. Those who walk in darkness enjoy living in sin. They only want to satisfy the lusts of the flesh.

"Now the works of the flesh are evident, which are: adultery, fornication, uncleanness, lewdness, idolatry, sorcery, hatred, contentions, jealousies, outbursts of wrath, selfish ambitions, dissensions, heresies, envy, murders, drunkenness, revelries, and the like; of which I tell you beforehand, just as I also told you in time past, that those who practice such things will not inherit the kingdom of God."

Galatians 5:19-21

But, those who are walking in His light are living their lives to bring glory to Him. They are fulfilling the God-given purpose they were born for, loving Him and loving people, seeking Him in prayer, reading His Word, worshiping, and sharing the hope of Christ Jesus with those who are living in darkness.

True Christians are all about having an intimate relationship with their Creator, sharing with others the hope that lies within them: God's love. Their hearts are full of His love, joy, peace, hope, contentment, and Eternal Life. These attributes are known as the fruit of the Spirit.

"But the fruit of the Spirit is love, joy, peace, longsuffering, kindness, goodness, faithfulness, gentleness, self-control. Against such there is no law. And those who are Christ's have crucified the flesh with its passions and desires. If we live in the Spirit, let us also walk in the Spirit. Let us not become conceited, provoking one another, envying one another."

Galatians 5:22-26

Please hear the urgency of this message, and call on the name of Jesus. He is the only way into the kingdom and to God, the Father. None of us are guaranteed our next breath, don't wait until you hear Jesus say, "Depart from Me, I never knew you." It will be too late.

I love you and don't want to see anyone go to hell. Jesus loves you so much He died for you and me so we could have eternal life. That we could be with Him, our Creator God, who created us in our mother's womb, and numbered the hairs we have on our heads. He gave us life and wants us to live it eternally with Him on Earth and in Heaven. Check your heart and call on Him, join in the family, so you too can fulfill your life-given purpose and destiny. He's waiting for you.

"Oh, taste and see that the Lord is good; Blessed is the man who trusts in Him!"

Psalms 34:8

THE GOOD SHEPHERD

The Lord is my Shepherd, He helps me to see,
He leads and guides me, He loves loving me.
I was like a lost sheep who had gone astray,
I wandered so hopelessly and went my own way.

I separated from the rest of the flock,
I'd scorn them, condemn them, and even mock.
It made me feel big to make them feel small,
I was being deceived by the deceiver of all.

I was first lured in by a suggestion or thought,
Then, as I took the bait, like a fish, I was caught.
With bitterness and anger growing inside of me,
I was bound up in sin, yet unable to see.

I was being consumed when I cried, "Lord, help me!"
"Please ease my pain and set me free!"
His rod and His staff they brought comfort my way.
The Lord is my Shepherd and He's with me to stay.

If you're like a lost sheep who has gone astray,
Cry out to The Shepherd, He's here today,
To wash you and cleanse you from all of your sins.
He will open your eyes when you let Him in.

Surely goodness and mercy will follow you,
In all that you say and do.
When you ask Him into your heart,
You can have a brand new start.

Dear Father in Heaven, forgive me,
I ask You to come into my heart.
To cleanse me from all of my sins,
And give me a brand new start.

Please open my eyes and set me free,
So I can walk in victory!
I give you my struggles and my strife,
And accept Your gift of Eternal Life.

I thank You for dying on Calvary,
So that I can come to You and be set free.
My life is now Yours, please show me Your will,
I'll trust in You daily as I climb every hill.

Holy Spirit, please fill me with God's love and His grace,
Help others to see Jesus, as they look in my face.
I thank You, Lord Jesus, for changing my heart,
You've given me hope and a brand new start.
Amen!

If you prayed this prayer and truly meant it from your heart, God heard it and will move powerfully in your life. You will begin to feel and see things differently.

Things that you used to do you will no longer have a desire to do. You will be drawn to Him and have a desire to get to know Him through reading the Bible and praying. Prayer is having a conversation with God as if He were sitting next to you. He is with you always, never leaving you or forsaking you.

He will transform your life and show you His will, and His plans and purpose for creating you. He loves you and will reveal many things to you as you draw close and get to know Him. With His leading, find other strong believers to help you learn how to trust God and to look to Him for the answers you need in your life. This will enable you to walk in love and integrity before the One who loves and Created you, for such a time as this.

Matcine Pepper
Based on Psalm 23
August 25, 1998

DO YOU TRULY KNOW HIM

Have you heard the Good News? Are you filled with hope or hopelessness in all you see happening around us today? The Good News is no matter what tomorrow holds if we know Who holds tomorrow, we have nothing to fear. The key word is if we "know" Who holds tomorrow, not just know about Him.

It's not enough to know that Jesus died on the cross to save us from our sins, He desires an intimate relationship with us. You can't truly know someone who is just a casual acquaintance. If you only go to Him when times are hard, or you're struggling and need a "quick fix," let's be honest, my friend, do you truly know Him?

Have you ever had a friend or family member you hear from only when they need something? It's not a pleasant feeling. You know that person doesn't value you but is only using you for their benefit. Imagine how Jesus might feel if we come to Him only to ask for help. If you could ever grasp what joy and peace are in store for your life, you would want to know Him. He will show you just how valuable you are to Him.

You will never feel worthless, unloved, or used in your relationship with Jesus. When I finally realized Jesus is the only One I can trust with my heart, I began trusting Him. I quit calling out to Him just for things I wanted or needed. Instead, I began to thank Him for His presence in my life, His hand of protection and favor upon me, and all of His many blessings. I started getting to know Him through His Word.

The Bible, God's inspired Word, is how you can truly get to know Him. For any challenge we face in life, His Word is all we need. It is God-breathed, and written for us. Spoken by His Spirit to men He set apart to express His heart and will, it is alive and active as we apply its truths to our lives. It will quench the fiery darts of the enemy and dispel every lie he speaks to you as God's Word settles into your heart.

Other ways to get to know Him are through worship, prayer, and thanksgiving. As you spend time worshiping Him either through song or magnifying His name in praise, you are taking the focus off yourself, your problems and needs, and giving Him the honor He is due!

When your focus is on Him and you no longer feel bogged down with your burdens, it's as if the heavens open up for you. You are now touching His heart, and He will begin moving upon you by His Spirit. You are no longer being controlled by your selfish nature, you are touching Him with your spirit. It is now a Spirit-to-spirit exchange. You will often sense His tangible presence when this happens and may be overcome with emotions such as deep feelings of love and peace, often with tears. There is a washing and a cleansing taking place during these times. Just spend precious time in His presence and let Him bring healing and restoration to you. This heightened awareness of His presence is also known as being in the Secret Place. A place where He can impart wisdom, revelation, dreams, visions, and many special encounters you might not otherwise experience.

Ask Him to explain things in His Word you don't understand, and to expose anything in your heart hindering you from walking in freedom. When He does expose a mindset contrary to His heart for you, turn away from those things through repentance, asking Him to forgive you. You will continue to receive more healing and deliverance from the clutches of the enemy, as you learn to walk in the victory of the Cross, and the Blood of Jesus.

I began to find out not only Who He is in me, but also who I am in Him. He expressed His unconditional love and forgiveness for me in ways I had never experienced before. Had He changed? No, it was I who was changed by His grace. For the first time in my life, I knew I loved Him and He loves me. But, beyond that, I was able to look in the mirror and finally feel love for the person I was looking at in the reflection. Jesus loves me, so I can love myself!

Through the blood of Christ, and an intimate relationship with Him, my life has been transformed, and, if you want, He will transform yours too! If you will only surrender your doubts and trust Him, He will show you

He loves you as you are. Then His love and presence will begin your transformation. Before long, you will see a more peaceful, loving, kind, and secure image in the mirror. When you know He is breaking the chains that have kept you bound, you will see yourself differently. The caterpillar becomes the butterfly. He brings to life what once seemed dead.

Even with our best intentions, there is nothing we can do in our power to earn God's grace or forgiveness. Jesus paid the price for our freedom and only He can restore our lives, giving us hope and a future worth living. He has secured our eternal destiny. All we have to do is repent of our sins, surrender our lives to Him, and give Him full control. Don't look at it as what you are giving up, but see it as what you are gaining: life in His kingdom of joy and peace, becoming all that He has made you to be, fulfilling the dreams He has for you, and spending the rest of eternity in His presence and glory.

"Oh, taste and see that the Lord is good; Blessed is the man who trusts in Him!"

Psalms 34:8

"And they overcame him (satan) by the blood of the Lamb and by the word of their testimony, and they did not love their lives to the death."

Revelation 12:11

"Now by this we know that we know Him, if we keep His commandments. He who says, "I know Him,"

and does not keep His commandments, is a liar, and the truth is not in Him. But whoever keeps His word, truly the love of God is perfected in him. By this we know that we are in Him."

1 John 2:3-5

FINAL THOUGHTS

I want to thank you, dear reader, for endeavoring to discover Do I Truly Know Him. Writing this book has been an intense labor of love for you from God our Father, and also from me.

The encouraging words, poems, and prophecies were inspired by the Holy Spirit to help us all seek Him in a more intimate way. The testimonies are my personal experiences throughout my life. They are meant to bring encouragement and hope to all; if He uses the tests in my life and turns them into a testimony of praise to Him, He will do the same for you!

My life is far from perfect but is being perfected daily by Him as I submit and surrender my will to His will. He will do the same for everyone who calls on His name and trusts Him for every need.

As you go from just knowing about Him to truly knowing Him, God will supersede every dream and expectation you could ever have of Who He actually is. Yes,

Final Thoughts

He is God our Creator and is to be reverenced. He is also Abba, meaning Father, Papa, or Daddy. He is a personal God and wants us to trust Him beyond what seems natural. He is Supernatural; our finite minds can't fully grasp Him. This is why we are told to have faith. Faith is not meant to be fully understood, as God's thoughts are higher than our thoughts, and His ways are higher than our ways. Just let go and trust He will guide your every step as you lay it all down for Him.

This has been a healing journey for me. I know His hand and anointing are upon the words in this book to bring deep inner healing to all who read it. I pray you will reflect on each entry and search the Word of God to get even greater insight, using the scriptures I referenced as a springboard.

As you walk away from reading this book of hope, I pray the revelation will be completely settled in your heart so that you too can say, "Yes, I do truly know Him." This book is not meant to be a substitute for reading God's Word but an encouragement to seek Him even more. As you read the Word and grow in your understanding and knowledge of God, you will grow stronger in your daily walk. Then you can honestly say, "I do truly know Him, and not just about Him."

May God's grace, peace, and blessings overflow in your life. May His light shine brightly as you go forth proclaiming the goodness and mercy of God to those who don't yet know Him, and might not even know about Him. Share the hope that lies within you, so they too can truly know Him. In Jesus' name I pray, Amen.

[1] encyclopeadia.com
[2] thefreedictionary.com

You have a story.
We want to publish it.

Everyone has as a story to tell. It might be about something you know how to do, or what has happened in your life, or it may be a thrilling, or romantic, or intriguing, or heartwarming, or suspenseful story, starring a cast of characters that have been swimming around in your imagination.

And at Wyatt & Sons Publishers, we can get your story onto the pages of a book just like the one you are holding in your hand. With professional interior design and a custom, professionally designed cover built just for you from the start, you can finally see your dream of being an author become reality. Then, you will see your book listed with retailers all over the world as people are able to buy your book from wherever they are and have it delivered to their home or their e-reader.

So what are you waiting for? This is your time.

visit us at
www.wyattpublishing.com
for details on how to get started becoming a
published author right away.

www.ingramcontent.com/pod-product-compliance
Lightning Source LLC
LaVergne TN
LVHW041336080426
835512LV00006B/490